Leading Magnanimously

# LEADING MAGNANIMOUSLY

## The Power of Heart, Trust, and Intent...

---

### ANDREW BRUMMER

NEW YORK

LONDON • NASHVILLE • MELBOURNE • VANCOUVER

# LEADING MAGNANIMOUSLY

## The Power of Heart, Trust, and Intent in Leading Teams

© 2025 Andrew Brümmer

All rights reserved. No portion of this book may be reproduced, stored in a retrieval system, or transmitted in any form or by any means—electronic, mechanical, photocopy, recording, scanning, or other—except for brief quotations in critical reviews or articles, without the prior written permission of the publisher.

Published in New York, New York, by Morgan James Publishing. Morgan James is a trademark of Morgan James, LLC. www.MorganJamesPublishing.com

For information about this title or to order other books and/or electronic media, please contact the publisher. Author: author@leadingmagnanimously.com.

Proudly distributed by Publishers Group West®

A **FREE** ebook edition is available for you or a friend with the purchase of this print book.

CLEARLY SIGN YOUR NAME ABOVE

**Instructions to claim your free ebook edition:**
1. Visit MorganJamesBOGO.com
2. Sign your name CLEARLY in the space above
3. Complete the form and submit a photo of this entire page
4. You or your friend can download the ebook to your preferred device

ISBN 9781636986715 paperback
ISBN 9781636986722 ebook
Library of Congress Control Number: 2025936973

**Cover Design by:**
Andrew Brummer

**Interior Design by:**
Chris Treccani
www.3dogcreative.net

Morgan James is a proud partner of Habitat for Humanity Peninsula and Greater Williamsburg. Partners in building since 2006.

Get involved today! Visit: www.morgan-james-publishing.com/giving-back

## COPYWRITE RECOGNITION

This book references content available on various websites, including YouTube, TED and TEDx Talks, Wikipedia, quote collections, individual authors' pages, URLs, and movies. All links are provided to direct readers straight to the relevant content—such as videos, books, or pages—with no alterations, tracking, or redirects by the author. This is intended to simplify access to the referenced material.

Notable quote sources include *The Shawshank Redemption*, Andrew Carnegie, Lao Tzu, and Theodore Roosevelt. Book references, quotes, or inferences draw from works like Stephen Covey's *The Seven Habits of Highly Effective People*.

All content, marks, inferences, and their associated user interfaces or features are proprietary to their respective creators or websites. Trademarks and content mentioned in this book belong to their respective owners. Their inclusion here is solely for informational and reference purposes, facilitating access to the cited material.

*To my mom, Ann, for teaching me how to lead.*

*To my dad, Hans, for teaching me how to work.*

*Thank you!*

*To my team members, I love you!*

# ACKNOWLEDGMENTS

To my teams–Past and Present–I love you.

To Laurie for giving me the space and latitude to demonstrate values and approaches work in LifeQ.

To Nina, for challenging me the way you do, the inflection and reflection platform you provide. For editing this document, and words of care you have given.

To all those who read the book and gave me feedback–specifically Belinda, Samantha, and Vanessa.

The all of the authors who have inspired me–in no order - Peter Drucker, Simon Sinek, Brian Tracy, James Clear, Kerry Patterson, Joseph Grenny, David Maxfield, Stephen Covey, Adam Grant, Brene Brown to name a few. The words you have written have helped me shape how I lead, the approaches I have taken, the confidence I have executed against.

To Anri for the guidance on the art, the collection and branding.

# FOREWORD

I enjoy debating Andrew. We do it weekly, if not daily. Even when we have diametrically opposed views on a topic, we speak our minds, share unfiltered opinions, and leave nothing unsaid. There are no elephants in the room. Nothing is off the table. Through sharpening each other's thinking, engaging in give-and-take, and challenging each other, we consistently leave candid discussions with a common goal and clear path forward. And we've undoubtedly shared some laughs along the way.

Andrew's leadership thrives in this space of honest, direct conversations. He doesn't shy away from difficult debate or conflict. Instead, he stands in its firing line, learning from it and using it as a tool to inspire growth and change in both himself and others.

In fostering these moments of honest heart-to-hearts, Andrew sets himself apart with the loyalty and respect he inspires. This is a testament to his leadership style — one that prioritizes integrity, trust, and connection. I've seen firsthand how his former colleagues, even those impacted by difficult decisions, continue to hold him in high regard and would jump at the chance to work with him again.

In this book, Andrew invites you into that same kind of unfiltered dialogue. As I read, I could hear his voice, as I've experienced it first-hand working directly with him. This is not a book of abstract ideas or high-level platitudes detached from reality. It is a hands-on guide to leadership, rooted in Andrew's personal journey and his years of experience leading from the trenches. Each section offers practical insight and actionable strategies, honed through real-world application and a willingness to adapt and grow.

Consider this book your invitation to rethink how you lead. It's a blueprint to build independent teams that thrive under your guidance. To lead with authenticity, heart, and intent. To be a magnanimous leader.

Nina Uys

*To be is to do.*
—SOCRATES

*"Do you use your people to do work,
or do you do the work with your people?*

# INTRODUCTION

## The Magnanimous Leader

Explore how to become your unique version of a magnanimous leader, where your team members are eager to work with you and stand by you through the ups and downs of the company. Being Magnanimous is within arm's reach; you just have to want it.

Imagine having a team that, despite the odds, is committed to working with you. Picture yourself taking a two-week holiday and returning to find that all administrative tasks, deliverables, and decisions have been handled smoothly. Envision a team that embodies the mission and cause as clearly as you would, even in your absence.

Imagine not needing to be present at team meetings to discuss deliverables, timelines, or conflicts. Visualize a team that feels safe to challenge your ideas and approaches, a team that agrees and disagrees constructively with you, and executes what the team and company need.

Imagine a team that understands your strengths and weaknesses and instinctively covers your weaknesses. Picture never having to worry about being undermined by your team, knowing they are in perfect alignment with you.

Imagine, for financial reasons, you have to downsize your team, and after the downsize they still want to return and work with you despite the life-changing events they faced—and when you bring them back, it was like they never left!

Imagine a team that is dedicated to ensuring they are managed and led by you and will do everything in their power to make it happen.

*I experience this with my team.*
*What will your leadership legacy be?*

## Words from the Author

This book is not theory bound. I have not based it on any human management philosophies, beliefs, or formal constructs. This book stems directly from my experiences as a leader, how I have chosen to lead, how I have created teams that are fundamentally different. This is introspection. Take from this that which resonates with you.

I focused this book on practicalities you can start implementing today. Being a magnanimous leader and having a stellar team around you is within arm's reach for you to grab hold of. I have broken this book into six sections so you can easily come back to the various parts when you need them.

"Cornerstones" focuses on the foundations I believe are present in any magnanimous team. This includes an autonomous team that is self-sustaining and able to operate without you, the leader, being around. This requires a high level of trust where people say what they mean, mean what they say, and do what they say they will do. The team members will operate without being worried about what is being said or agreed on without them present, where intent is pervasively known, clear, and shared across the team. They will have a sense of loyalty to one another at a personal and professional level, toward you their leader, and toward the company. They will also have a level of passion that is self-sustaining and brings out levels of personal care and love for the team and mission.

"Fundamentals" focuses on some organizational dynamics that will make it very hard for you. While I recognize that these are present in any organization, calling them what they are is like touching the elephant in the room: it makes them a speakable topic. These will not stop or hinder you, but wrapping your head around how to address these will be critical. These include workplace alignment around mission, cause, and priorities; workplace politics; psychological safe places; and your participation in meetings.

"To Be . . . or Not?" focuses on leadership characteristics that I believe have helped me be successful. While not all-encompassing, these are a subset

I have seen help any manager become a magnanimous leader. In these, you will find characteristics that are simple for you to realize, though some will be harder than others. Take your small wins and strive to demonstrate as many of these characteristics as you can, and where you cannot, draw people in around you who are able to fill in the gaps. Remember, we win together. I have included several references in each section here that will be available as a download if you have purchased the printed copy.

"Working with your Team" focuses on using these concepts as you engage with your team. Having the characteristics is very different from practicing them, let alone being effective or proficient in the use thereof. In this section, you will find several cross-references to the "To Be . . . or Not?" section and how to leverage these characteristics in situations. It also includes some basic things you can do with your team to help them grow and to drive yourself toward being magnanimous.

In "Let Them . . ." I encourage you to take risks with your team. It will take them a while to get it right, and at first, it will likely be chaotic. There are some things they have to experience and develop skills in that will enable success. If you prevent them from experiencing this, you will end up having the proverbial monkey on your back: you will own the problems, and the team will not be able to function effectively without you being present.

> *"Andrew, it's impossible to tell you just how differently our team operates and engages under your leadership in comparison to the other teams in the company. It is so different, on so many levels."*
> **—A TEAM MEMBER**

Lastly, I close with "Don'ts . . ." There are some things you just cannot do as a leader, some simple rules you must follow.

I trust you will find your path through here and discover your own version of leadership magic in getting your team to want to be led by you. In doing so, you will bring out the magnanimous parts of your leadership story that will leave an echo in your team members and how they lead people, which will then impact team members beyond that, which none of us will get to experience. Just how great are you going to be?

## Independent Teams

Independent teams are the most powerful representation of the collective of humans. They have deep organizational insights, awareness of the mission, ability to execute as a single human unit, and a deep sense of loyalty for another and the company.

These teams are company aware, leader aware, and market aware and have a clear sense of purpose. Their alignment with one another and their mission helps ensure they are continuously working together toward a common set of outcomes and objectives. This fosters a deep sense of unity and direction.

These teams are structurally, procedurally, and strategically aligned and follow well-defined, though not necessarily industry, frameworks. This approach facilitates effective change and challenge navigation without the need for constant supervision or micro-management. They are equipped with resources and skills that facilitate execution while ensuring strategic intent and plans are implemented smoothly and on time.

Independent teams do not require hand-holding or continuous oversight. They thrive on trust, empowerment, innovation, problem-solving, and rapid adaption to the changing environment and business, fostering accountability, ownership, and personal responsibility.

These teams can be left to their own devices and make significant progress. They are self-sufficient, self-driven, proactive, and strive toward excellence as a collective. While boosting productivity, these characteristics enhance individual and collective job satisfaction, engagement among team members, personal values, and a cohesive environment that delivers results.

## My Journey

I have learned many lessons throughout my years of leadership, facilitated by many experiences, that have shaped the way I lead. My journey has taken me from banking, activity-based costing, software development, and product management, to organizational change, consulting, business process optimization, sales, human resources, operations, and the executive office.

I have morphed and evolved my leadership style as expectations and societal norms have evolved over the years. These lessons have become my guiding principles and have helped me develop a set of tenets and rules that I live and lead by. I continually introspect on what's not working and why (Why could I not reach that person?) and challenge myself to be better, to evolve and grow, and I am constantly growing—often intentionally diving into the pit of leadership and/organizational dysfunction to grab the bull by the proverbial horns. I have made sure to always stick to these principles as my foundation of the leadership style—consistency, fairness, and humanity are pivotal.

I am a Leader-Doer, not a Doer-Leader. This means I lead first; everything is about making sure that the people reporting to me know what they need to do. My job is to get stuff out of their way and be their council. I make it abundantly clear that I am an ear, a shoulder, a mind, a coach, and a challenge wall for ideation and novel thinking. I am here to help them think, work, and decide without me. My job as an effective leader is that of a multiplier—I am NOT here to do their job. The quicker and more efficiently they do their job without me, the better and faster we multiply and scale.

I stay as focused on the rules of "the why," leading into "the what" as much as possible. That means I attempt to give high-level rules or boundaries of business priorities and help them figure out what the details are—with the goal of them being able to figure it out without me. I cannot overemphasize the importance of this: I teach them to understand the principles and business rationale that facilitates the what and the why, and by doing this, I mega-multiply their critical thinking ability, especially when I'm not around.

Next is making sure they are in full control of how work is done. This means NOT, in any way, pre- or post-ordaining how the work should be done, unless something catastrophic is about to go wrong (i.e., business impacting). This often means allowing the team, in its infancy, to fail safely on small projects and activities. Like learning to be a parent, there are guidelines and macro rules one should parent by, and the details are learned daily. The quicker they can learn, the faster I can scale and get out of their way. Yes, this is counter-intuitive, I know. But they need to function without me—my job is to teach them and hold them accountable to execute.

Now, it is important to know that they will not learn as fast as you would like. They will be stubborn. They will wait to be told or micro-managed; they will unwittingly wait for you. It will take many stabs, many months to get them to become self-aware and to bond and start executing. Be patient!!!

Because of the Doer side in me, I keep as much crap work away from my team as possible. This means everything that I perceive as rubbish work or not related to their job functions. My team has coined me "Chief of All the Things No One Wants to Do."

A Doer Leader is exactly the opposite, doing tasks first and then leading. Typically, a team reporting to a Doer Leader feels they are left out of novel, exciting projects, or micromanaged, being told how to do what they are doing and being scolded for having initiative. The leader in this function is typically a knowledge, execution, and human growth bottleneck—and most of the time does not know it or will fight to remain in denial.

An important realization is that leadership is a constantly evolving concept. I have made a conscious effort to stay up to date with a flexible mindset when taking charge. It's a continuous process of learning, growing, and seeking new avenues to support team members to become integral parts of a larger, self-aware, and socially conscious unit.

My journey of leadership has been a constant learning experience. I have faced challenges, made mistakes, and celebrated successes, and through it all I have remained true to the people around me, true to my foundations of being human with humans. These tenets and rules have helped me create a positive and productive work environment for teams I have been part of. I am proud of the leader I have become, and the one I will grow into tomorrow.

I make no claims to possess all knowledge, nor do I assume that my methods will suit everyone. Within these pages, I have compiled the techniques I use to lead, with the dream that they will inspire others to become exceptional enablers in their own unique ways. You must always be on, always full of energy and inspiration. You, for the most part, must always be a glass overflowingly full. You need to inspire people to want: to want something more, something different, to stretch the extra mile.

I had one client who pulled me aside years ago and said, "Andrew, the team is doing very well, the project is back on track despite the odds, and deliverables are being met, but your name is not on any of them." I politely smiled and said, "I know, that's why you hired me. When I'm gone, this activity will stay alive because of the people who now own it, not because I did it." To the best of my knowledge, that activity is still kicking and screaming inside the walls of the company fifteen-plus years later.

In Italy Talgam's[1] talk on leadership where he uses differing orchestra conductors' approaches to create a visual of leadership, the last conductor's reference paints a leadership style I strive to attain—"doing without doing." All this conductor does is sit back and enjoy the execution. *Please take the time to watch this.*

In all areas where I have been allowed to lead the way I do, we, the team, have experienced near euphoria. It's not all about parties and dreaming. It is possible to create environments that yield the most incredible teams and people, who can scale, expand, represent, and be the company without you having to guard.

I have written this with the intent of putting some practical, simple, small things you can use toward your journey of creating your version of being magnanimous. Who will you find in these pages? Which of these have you always known and not yet put together?

I am an avid reader, with hundreds of books in my audio library—many of them I have listened to many times. I have added a key set of reads at the end of this book.

### "What's your version of being a Magnanimous Leader?

---

[1] The TED talk is on YouTube "Itay Talgam: Lead like the great conductors" at minute 19:26 (https://www.youtube.com/watch?v=R9g3Q-qvtss&ab_channel=TED) - The conductor has clearly spent so much time and effort working with the team - they execute without him doing anything.

*Remember, we each have come to be who we are through the stories of our life that no one knows. We have each woven a fabric of ourselves which, for each of us, is the perfect representation of who we are today. Your job as a leader is to love that woven fabric of every individual, in the unique way each fabric wants to and allows itself to be loved.*

# CORNERSTONES

These cornerstones are some fundamental attributes/states that will inevitably be present in any high-performing team. They are states or observations you will see or experience from a well-functioning team.

These principles exist as a result of magnanimous leaders who create an environment where team members feel valued, motivated, and capable of achieving great things. These qualities help you build a resilient, innovative, and high-performing team that drives organizational success.

## Autonomy
*The team will be autonomous!*

Autonomous, edge mandate, and self-managed teams are based on the idea that individual team members are given the freedom, space, and clarity of objectives to make decisions and take actions without constant supervision. This results in a flexible and efficient work environment where collective and unique contributions to the success of the team can rise. This promotes ownership and accountability, as teams and team members think and decide for themselves and own their actions, decisions, and approaches, enabling solutions and keeping the company informed.

Ownership encourages team members to take initiative and manage responsibility for their tasks and projects. Individuals who experience this sense of ownership are more likely to put in the effort required to achieve and exceed outcomes. Self-accountability has team members holding themselves responsible for actions, decisions, and deadlines; maintaining quality standards; and adhering to agreed processes.

Teams are, through collective decision-making, empowered regarding their projects. This ensures all team members have a say in the direction and execution, leading to innovative solutions. Team members get to collectively decide on the best approaches, including planning, milestones, roles, and responsibilities.

Autonomy works when there are regular progress updates into the broader organization covering challenges and successes. This transparency builds trust, ensuring alignment with goals and objectives. Open communication channels allow for continuous feedback across the company, continuously striving to identify areas for improvement and achievement celebration.

Team members that feel this sense of ownership and accountability are more engaged and motivated, resulting in higher productivity and job satisfaction. These teams tend to perform better, are more agile, adapt to changes quicker, and deliver high-quality results. Empowered teams are more likely to experiment and innovate through creative problem-solving and the development of new ideas.

*Autonomy* is the level of control and independence team members have within their work, not limited to decisions, goals, time management, and resources. This leads to improved motivation and creativity through empowerment. The *edge mandate* describes the boundaries of a team or team members, clarifying which decisions and actions individuals are responsible for and which require input from others. This facilitates more efficient decision-making and promotes team and team member accountability.

Self-managed teams work together to achieve a common goal without the need for a traditional manager. These teams are founded on trust, communication, and collaboration in decision-making. These make for a more adaptable and agile working environment with quick and efficient decisions without higher approval. Notably, these come with the associated responsibilities.

It is important these teams work within the company strategy and direction. While these concepts promise immense value, misuse can be catastrophic. Clear communication is critical, specifically the vision, mission, and strategic goals, ensuring the broader concepts are understood by everyone. This includes regular updates on company strategy through team meetings, company communications, and one-on-one sessions.

Team members should understand how individual objectives contribute to the team, as well as the company's strategic direction. Team goals should cascade from company objectives and create a clear link between team activities and the company strategy. Progress reviews are essential in ensuring the team is on track with their goals and that they remain aligned. Reviews should be used to refine any behavior or decisioning.

Providing and receiving feedback should be included in regular one-on-one and team meetings and with feedback tools that facilitate the sharing of insights and concerns. Empowering team members like this includes providing them with the necessary information, resources, and authority to make decisions within their scope of work. Communication platforms such as intranets, newsletters, All Hands, and/or town hall meetings should be used to communicate updates.

Frameworks that guide decision-making processes that ensure alignment are crucial and could include decision matrices and strategic planning tools, among other tools. Strategic communication checkpoints should be included in project plans.

Collaboration with other teams to ensure a unified approach is a necessity to keep the team's efforts integrated with broader initiatives, ensuring the individual team activities support the larger company initiatives.

When empowering your team, I have found agreeing on a set of social contracts that creates a binding behavioral expectation. This will allow you to interject where you experience discomfort in trajectory, as well as hold the team accountable for reaching out to you for guidance. My social contracts are simple:
- Be the servant, be human, always. You have no idea what the other person's life journey has been, in the past day, week, month, year, or lifetime.

- I am not here to do your job. If you don't know, let's talk. If you cannot, then we need to pivot and find a more suitable spot for you.
- Own what you do. Don't make excuses or point fingers. Remember, when pointing fingers, there are three coming back at you.
- Don't let me get caught with my pants down. I cannot help when I'm on the back foot; I cannot help you if I don't know

We want the teams to think for themselves, ideate by themselves, and execute within the mandate. Where the teams are faced with design, architectural, or procedural decisions that are significant and/or they are unsure of the path, goals, requirements, instructions, or where objectives are being "interpreted," the team should always default to clarification calls. Anyone knowingly proceeding further without this is just stupid!

Through your journey with the team, you must be pervasively and consistently clear on the underlying tenets that make the why. You must work tirelessly to prevent the "why" from becoming a blocker. I have found helping the team understand the tenets underneath the why, what rules and business decisions the whys are built on, helps them think for themselves. My goal is to help self-based critical thinking. This takes time to coach and a lot more than answering the why, but once it settles in, it is amazing. A core facilitator of this is transparency, covered in the "To Be . . . or Not?" section below.

I am in no way suggesting the team should have the right to change the direction of any product or decision because they don't agree with the why. Nor should the team be questioning every decision the company makes. Every team member has the privilege to introspect and decide if they do not align with the why and move on. You, as a leader, must not fight this.

How you handle these questions and ideas is vital—you can destroy all of your work toward the creation of a team in minutes. Remember, the goal is to get your team's critical thinking working.

This is the oxymoron: As humans, despite what most people say, we have an innate desire to be told what to do and how to do it. While there are many reasons for this, the limiting factors is we need approval from a higher authority. It gives us a sense of security and reassurance that we are on the right track.

Independence can be a daunting concept, especially when there is no one to make decisions and take responsibility for the outcome. The fear of failure and the unknown can hold us back from reaching our full potential. However, for those who, both leader and team member, are able to overcome this apprehension of relinquishing control, the possibilities are boundless. With autonomy comes the freedom to explore new ideas, take risks, and learn from our mistakes.

The concepts surrounding autonomy, edge mandate, and self-management are part of the cornerstones for loyalty to exist. When individuals are given the space and trust to make their own decisions, they feel a sense of ownership and pride in their work. This leads to a stronger commitment and dedication to their tasks, resulting in increased productivity and loyalty. It also fosters a culture of mutual respect and trust between team members and their higher authority. With autonomy, individuals are not just following orders, but actively contributing to the success of the organization.

## Trust
*There will be a very high level of trust!*

Team-based trust is a critical foundation of any successful company, a vital component in fostering positive, healthy relationships and effective communication. Trust is the belief and confidence in the reliability, truthfulness, and ability of someone or something.

Trust is essential for the smooth functioning of teams working to achieve company goals. With trust, team members naturally feel secure in their roles, knowing that the people around them, especially leadership, have their best interests at heart. This creates psychological safety, a state in which individuals take more risks, share ideas openly, and collaborate.

This trust is fundamental. Trust among peers encourages collaboration and provides that collaborative environment where team members are not afraid to talk, ideate, make mistakes, or ask for help, knowing that support is inevitable and judgment is absent.

Trust between team members and leaders is critically important; demonstration of trust by delegating tasks without micromanaging empowers ownership.

Trust between team members and the company is crucial for job satisfaction and retention. This demonstrates that the company values their team's well-being and career growth, driving further commitment and loyalty. Trust between the leader and the company is vital for organizational cohesion, and leaders who trust the vision are better equipped to inspire and guide their teams effectively.

To achieve this, companies must foster a culture of transparency, honesty, and respect, ensuring that trust is valued and nurtured at all levels. Trust also plays a crucial role in communication; team members are more likely to be open and transparent.

Trust promotes teamwork and effective communication and strengthens relationships between team members, their leaders, and the company. Fostering a culture of transparency, honesty, and respect, companies will ensure trust is nurtured at all levels.

I have used the book *"The Speed of Trust"* by *Stephen M. R. Covey* in many instances where trust is fundamentally broken. I have distributed this book through the company's affected teams. It covers how trust is built one step at a time, one micro action at a time. There is no silver bullet.

Trust is hard to earn and easy to lose. Loyalty cannot be found where trust is absent!

*Say what you mean, mean what you say,
do what you say you are going to do.*

### Intent

*There will be a clear alignment and understanding of individual intent!*

Intent is the underlying motivation or purpose behind a person's actions or words. It is the driving force behind their behavior and the reason for their communication. Intent can be conscious or subconscious, and it can vary depending on the individual and the situation.

I choose to believe that people's intent is always pure and comes from a genuine place. Yes, some have argued that intent can be manipulative or selfish. I believe people are inherently good and have positive intentions. Poor decisions do not equate to bad intentions. There is often no clear right or wrong answer when it comes to understanding someone's intent—it is how the observer experiences that intent, with all they know about the person and the company, matched to their own.

Intent can be selfish and manipulative, words and actions with the sole objective to achieve personal gain and/or manipulate others. In my experience, people are not stupid. Intent is like the smell of yesterday's burnt toast—it is self-evident and will always present its truth—sometimes sooner than later—and when one is found to be of poor intent, recovery will be hard, trust will be absent, and loyalty cannot be present.

*Intent* plays a crucial role in determining trust in any relationship or interaction. It refers to the purpose or motivation behind someone's actions, and it greatly impacts how others perceive and interpret those actions. In the context of trust, intent can either strengthen or weaken it, depending on whether it aligns with the expectations and beliefs of the person being trusted.

If someone's intent is perceived as positive, genuine, and well-meaning—in their eyes—it is more likely to build trust. For instance, if a friend offers to help without any ulterior motives or hidden agendas, their intent is seen as pure and trustworthy. Similarly, if a company's intent is to provide quality products and services to its customers, it can build a strong sense of trust and loyalty among its consumers. In both these scenarios, the intent is aligned with the expectations and needs of the person being trusted, thus strengthening the bond of trust.

On the other hand, if someone's intent is perceived as negative, deceitful, or self-serving, it can significantly damage trust. For example, if a person is caught lying or manipulating others for their benefit, their intent is seen as untrustworthy and can lead to a breakdown of trust in that relationship. Similarly, if a company's intent is to maximize profits at the expense of its customers' well-being, it can result in a loss of trust and reputation.

Intent is my number one measure of someone, anyone, regardless of my interactions or purposeful trajectory with that person. Intent tells everything—the beauty of it is that it is presented in small ways, hundreds of them, many of which we have no idea we are broadcasting. While it may be forced and fake to start, malintent will always eventually show itself.

The reasons for this is your intentions as a leader must be clear, consistent, and honest. Your team will know when you are manipulating for self-gain or agenda-driven reasons. Your team cannot develop loyalty if they do not understand your intent-if your intent is not aligned with the individual, the team, or company mission.

This does not mean your intent must be angelic. It means, don't hide your intentions. The teams that are aligned with your intent, regardless thereof, with the right behaviors, will be loyal, deeply passionate, and engaged—they will be magnanimous.

## Loyalty

*There will be a high sense of loyalty to one another, the team, and the leader!*

The team's loyalty to the team, to you, and by implication to the company, is a cornerstone of any successful company. *Loyalty*, at its core, refers to a strong, unwavering dedication, a highly valued quality sought after in relationships, companies, and communities.

Loyalty is being faithful and devoted to someone, a friend, family member, romantic partner, or oneself. It involves standing by that person through good and bad, supporting them, and keeping their best interests in mind. A loyal friend will not abandon you when things get tough, and a loyal team member will always act in the best interest of the team. Loyalty encompasses trust and honesty.

Loyalty is a sense of duty/obligation toward a person, group, company, cause, or nation; being committed to its goals and values; and actively contributing to its success. This is often seen in the military and on sports teams. An example is when team members are deeply committed to the company's mission and values and continuously go the extra mile, or a team member works extra hours to meet critical deadlines or solve complex problems.

Loyalty has negative connotations and consequences when loyalty becomes blind and unquestioning. This can be seen in toxic relationships or blind allegiance to an authority figure or ideology. For instance, following a manager's directives even when those directives are unethical or harmful. It is important to examine the object of loyalty and ensure it aligns with our personal values and beliefs.

Loyalty is multifaceted and encompasses dedication, trust, and duty. It manifests in various forms and is an essential quality in building and maintaining strong relationships. It is crucial to examine and evaluate the object of our loyalty to ensure that it is deserving and aligns with our personal values.

Loyalty is undoubtedly the linchpin to successful teams. This quality cannot be purchased or obtained through employment; it cannot be bought, interviewed for, or performance reviewed. It is a quality that is earned and nurtured over time. Loyalty cannot be forced or demanded; it must be willingly given. It is a rare and precious trait cultivated in an environment where individuals are motivated to take ownership of their work and strive toward the greater good. In a nurturing work environment, team members develop loyalty through positive experiences, fair treatment, and a shared sense of purpose based on trust.

In a world where people are often focused on personal gain and success, loyalty stands out as a shining beacon of hope: people willing to put the needs of others above their own and witness the greatness of their colleagues while being inspired to be a part of something greater than themselves.

We all have a deep desire to be a part of something meaningful and worthwhile, and loyalty creates bonds and connections. It is the glue that, along with trust, holds teams and/organizations together, the driving force behind many successful endeavors. Loyalty is incredibly subjective for the team member, the team, and you—the leader. Loyalty is complex and presents itself in odd ways, for odd reasons. What may be perfectly logical for me may be absolutely trite for you. Loyalty, indeed, is the precursor to passion.

Rich autonomy, deep trust, absolutely aligned intent, and loyalty come together within a common or shared cause. The missing ingredient is Passion.

## Passion
*The team will always go the extra mile; they will fight for and with one another to conquer all the odds against them!*

Passion is incredibly personal and intimate. It is an intense emotion or feeling toward a particular interest, activity, and/or goal—a drive that motivates us to pursue dreams, overcome obstacles, and push boundaries in the attainment of our full potential. Passion takes the form of creative pursuits, professional ambitions, and personal relationships; it influences many aspects of our lives.

Passion may be the pursuit of a creative outlet such as art, music, or writing, with you spending countless hours perfecting your craft, driven by an inner fire that ignites imagination. It's a dedication to conveying emotions and telling stories through creations.

Career-based passion may yield itself through the devotion of countless hours to work and constantly striving for success. Take software coding, where an engineer may spend long hours learning new languages, solving complex problems, and contributing to open-source projects. Their passion is clearly evident in their dedication and enthusiasm and sets them apart, ultimately leading to innovations that can transform industries.

Passion manifests itself in relationships, where individuals are deeply vested in one another and will go above and beyond to make their significant other happy and keep them safe. A passionate parent, for example, will tirelessly support their child's education and personal development, attend school events, help with homework, and nurture personal interests. This intense affection and connection drives them to continuously nurture and strengthen their bond with their child, resulting in a loving and supportive family environment.

Passion, a force that compels us to action, creates meaning in our lives. It gives us purpose and fulfillment and arrives in various forms throughout our lifetime. The holy grail of teamwork is passion! Where forces come together for a common cause, in the common pursuit of the team and company's mission. This bond transcends the ordinary, igniting a fire within us that cannot be contained. This passion requires trust, matched intent, loyalty, and personal ownership.

These teams are made up of a group of complex and intriguing characters, each bringing unique flavors to the mix, adding depth and dimension to the team, driven by a collective passion that is palpable, radiating from their every move and action.

Their chemistry is undeniable, a result of their unwavering commitment, an unbreakable bond that fuels their drive together. This chemistry can exist between team members and their leaders. On a sports team, for instance, trust and camaraderie among the players and coach are crucial. They train, strategize, and play together, each member understanding their role and contribution to the team's success. Through disagreements and conflicts, they unite like a tight-knit family, as one, when addressing the balance of the company.

Their journey toward success is about evoking strong emotions and leaving a lasting impression. This team understands and experiences the power of passion as a driving force to create a masterpiece, a shining example of what can be accomplished when individuals come together with a shared purpose.

As you watch these teams in action, you can't help but be drawn in by their character-rich voices. They speak with conviction and purpose, words laced with passion and determination. It is this passion that elevates them from good to great, making them an unstoppable force.

Thinking about the holy grail of team, think of this team: a group of individuals who share a collective passion for each other and their work. They are a living, breathing example of the power of passion and what can be achieved when it is harnessed. This passion-driven unity transforms their collective efforts into extraordinary achievements.

*"Play hard.
But first we work hard.
... and ...
always remember to play harder than you worked ...
... otherwise, what's the point!*

# ADDRESSING FUNDAMENTALS

We must attend to certain fundamental behavioral and/organizational dynamics. They are crucial for ensuring that team members do not feel stuck, alone in their efforts, or fighting a losing battle, left isolated on a hill.

Although it may not be possible to eliminate all of these challenges, it is imperative that your team experiences you as a champion who persists in addressing them. While not exhaustive, some of the behaviors you must proactively address include workplace synergy, internal dynamics, mental well-being, meeting approach, and workload interference.

## Workplace Alignment
*While not debilitating, lack thereof will create intense frustration!*

An effective, functioning company relies on executive alignment. This binds the organization together and propels it forward. Without this cohesion, chaos and aimlessness are bound to eventually ensue, either in dramatic fashion or through slow, benign areas of the company where putting a finger on the problem is nearly impossible. Regardless, the team will experience it in visceral ways. The micro-experiences between the executives are magnified the further away from the center it travels—picture a tsunami, the movement event, and the consequence onshore a thousand miles away.

I have spent eighteen years in organizational change and technology, where I have directly engaged in 70-plus companies and coached teams through problems in 350-plus companies. I have worked in Africa, Europe, the UK, Canada, and forty-seven states in the USA (not yet part of the Fifty Club). For years I have wondered why there is so much pervasive misalignment on the floor of a company, why the fiefdoms are how they have come to be, and why people cannot just step back and see the errors around them.

The light bulbs started turning on as I progressively moved into the executive suite over the last nine years. I circled with previous colleagues who also have risen to the executive suite; turns out this floor miss-alignment underpinned at the executive level is ever present. To my chagrin, this is glaringly obvious now. Let's leave this topic for another day, maybe another author.

Alignment is the cornerstone of success at the executive level, and at levels below the executives. The higher the alignment (or lack thereof), the more it defines culture and leadership. Alignment is important for steering choices and behaviors toward growth and expansion.

The scope for cultural and leadership alignment expands as alignment increases in the organizational framework. While you may not be able to have the skills or power to drive hard change toward company-wide alignment, your team must experience you to be driving toward alignment—at whatever level you are able to influence.

This is present in how you engage with your peers and the words you use to describe dysfunction in other parts of the company. It comes down to talking about the problem with intent to solve versus talking about it for self-justification, defense, or to minimize the person being spoken about. Do you speak with uplifting words, ideas, and thoughts, looking for answers, or do you speak with negativity, insinuating, "No can do."

Talking with your leads about these things are part of transparency, an important tool to help your team understand the innards of you, what your fiber is, what your intent is, why you are doing what you are doing, and what your targeted outcome is.

I have yet to work in a company where the alignment to cultural and leadership cause is ever present. Despite this, the fight and drive are worth it for the team, you and your company. Outside organizational change, consultants may well be the path you go to help expedite this. Remember, key with the consultants is they must leave behind the behaviors of change, not be the drivers of change. The latter will inevitably result in the company behavior returning to normal (pre their arrival).

I have worked in environments where there is absolutely no alignment, and over time—years—through demonstrating how to inspire and enable leaders, have slowly infected other teams who have joined the rally.

I am a firm believer, as a result of hard-earned experience, that common sense and passion are viral. People innately want these things, they innately want to believe and experience them, and when you make them possible, you will battle to stop the desire for more.

However, creating power-punch teams and alignment does not happen overnight. It can take years to get right. You, as the influencer, have to stay the course, be persistent, and demonstrate consistency in manner, mission, approach, and drive. It is possible, but it is hard. Seeing a power-punch team materialize is a phenomenal experience.

## Workplace Politics
*This will prevent your efforts from becoming viral, regardless of your team's success!*

The curveball in sustained expansive growth and adoption of passion is workplace politics, it specifically targets the counter to passion and cohesion. It drives division; suppresses voices, creativity, and ideas; and ostracizes.

Workplace politics includes the use of power and influence by individuals or groups within a workplace to achieve their own goals and objectives. It involves the complex interactions and dynamics between people in a professional setting, often with the aim of gaining advantages or advancing one's own agenda. This can include building alliances, forming cliques, and engaging in strategic maneuvering to gain favor and influence within the organization.

Workplace politics can also involve navigating hierarchies, managing conflicts, and making decisions based on personal relationships rather than objective criteria. Workplace politics can revolve around claims or ownership of work product or domain, people or product territory, personal intelligence, geographical proximity, founder connections, inner circles, or information. Workplace politics has at least two actors working against one another, and while tame initially, they can boil into life-long enemies.

While workplace politics is seen as a natural or even an inevitable aspect of any workplace, when taken to extreme levels, it can create a toxic and incredibly unhealthy work environment. However, some argue that it is an essential skill for success in the professional world, as it requires strong communication, negotiation, and interpersonal skills.

Here—you will have to choose. What I know is that trust, loyalty, and passion cannot thrive amidst workplace politics. While I understand workplace politics is ever-present, I do not believe it yields anywhere near the best out of people—it cannot ask for the extra mile, yield passion and a cohesive group, or provide a safe working environment. At a fundamental level, I do not believe it is needed or belongs. I have worked to call it and eliminate it as much as I am able—it is possible.

It is crucial to promptly recognize any discontentment and address the issues discreetly in small groups or, where needed, publicly. While it is possible to eliminate workplace politics, it requires some brave actions. Handling it may require you to put yourself in some very uncomfortable situations. Having a cohesive leadership team, at least the level you are, and consensus to sustain a positive culture will drastically increase the pace in addressing this.

The higher within the organizational stack alignment is achieved, the more probable it will be that you will be able to address workplace politics in a broader manner than your immediate sphere of influence. For smaller companies, this must be driven from the executive team, ideally the CEO—managed through the senior leadership team to middle management.

While massively advantageous for the executive team to initiate alignment, it is not a prerequisite for you to effectively eliminate workplace politics within the teams under your direct and indirect influence.

I have frequently been told that it cannot be eliminated; however, my personal experiences have been quite the contrary. As the one in charge, you need to decide, you must act, you must uphold a strict zero-tolerance stance toward it, and you must effectively communicate this to all members of your team. Swift and severe repercussions should ensue, including dismissal for those who violate this standard.

## Psychological Safe Space
*Safe space brings out the best in all of us!*

Psychological safe spaces are environments where individuals feel accepted, respected, and valued. I am a Gen-Xer, and I believe these safe spaces are vital if you want to bring out the best; promote communication, trust, and collaboration; and create an environment where people express their thoughts, feelings, and ideas without fear.

Safe spaces are more likely to yield listening and encourage healthy debates. These are destroyed when used as platforms to spread hate or intolerance toward others, creating a toxic environment.

Safe spaces are also destroyed when they are not properly maintained or managed, specifically if the people responsible for creating and maintaining that safety do not monitor and address issues, making safe spaces chaotic and ineffective in promoting healthy discussions.

Safe spaces require active participation and respecting the opinions and perspectives of others. Without this, they will become stagnant and fail to promote meaningful discussions. You are accountable for ensuring the strength and success and responsible for creating and nurturing these spaces, facilitating discussions and relationships.

Safe spaces are damaged and destroyed through small words and micro-actions. Your small words, tones, and body language are the most damaging; they happen without you knowing it. This is very hard to address because we are not aware we are doing it. Small things like the small raise of an eyebrow when someone proposes something, the gentle untimely tilt of the head when someone does something you consider stupid, the forehead frown when someone does something you don't agree with, the fidgeting of hands, moving to multi-task on email or some other computer productivity chore when on Zoom.

Examples of how well-intended phases that are over used destroy safe spaces (regardless of your intent) are as follows:
- "I hear what you're saying, but . . ."
- "I understand your perspective. However . . ."
- "Interesting point, but have you considered . . ."
- "That's a valid opinion, yet . . ."
- "I see where you're coming from, but . . ."
- "I appreciate your thoughts, but . . ."
- "While I respect your viewpoint . . ."
- "I can see why you feel that way, but . . ."
- "That's an interesting take, but . . ."

When we use these words over long periods of time, we create an unmistakable message that, "You do not know what you are doing. Let me give you the answers." While we believe we are helping, we are basically telling the person, "Shut up and do what I tell you."

I am not saying we should be banned from phrases like these. I am saying that if you use these types of phrases on a regular basis, you undermine yourself as a leader, you squash creative juices and the desire to speak up, and you collapse safe spaces. Remember, we can apologize for large events and irrational, silly acts like over-stepping boundaries or overreacting—but these small behaviors, not so much. In Stephen Covey's book *The 7 Habits of Highly Effective People*, he shares a powerful story about his son, who once said to him, "You are not sorry." Your team will view you in the same light—and your "sorry" will be irrelevant.

## Small Things

*Small are the ginormous things.*
*Get them wrong, and your efforts are mute!*

I cannot emphasize this enough: *Small things matter*!! I have experienced the smartest people I have known be socially illiterate—completely absent-minded of the importance of these things (this can be addressed) while believing they are doing the right things (not the damaging part) and choosing when they will try to save face and when they will continue engaging the way they have (the damaging part). I have also experienced it to the extreme: intentional and active, "I don't care, I am not their mother. If they are not going to do what I tell them, then they can #$%% off." While these are extremes, the first steps are for the leader to recognize their approaches and surround themselves with people who can help them through this—despite their bravado and pride. Without open-mindedness, inflection, and self-awareness, they will have to battle to overcome this.

> *Small things, small behaviors matter,*
> *and they must match words and intent.*

Small talk with your team matters! Small recognitions matter! Responding immediately matters! Letting them talk matters! Letting them fail matters! Birthday wishes matter! As you read through this, you will probably say, "Yes, yes, I know," but please introspect.

These examples of small things that matter are vastly more important and impactful than the project you just gave them ownership of. The project is a transactional activity. These small things are the glue that binds the fiber.

- Know their personal world, spouses' and children's names, hobbies, trials, tribulations, life events.
- Be a collective individual. Everyone is different. Treat and engage with them in ways that maximize them, not simplify you.
- Engage like you are a peer; let them know what's going on in the company, talk about it and life, talk about the problems to be solved, let them challenge you in private and public—they will do it respectfully.
- Show you care, listen. Stop talking or trying to one-up them. Let them finish their sentences, let them own the idea, shut up when they are done—let them close the discussion
- Their weak and poor moments are theirs. Be there for them, and do not minimize their experiences by telling them about yours.

- Respect their frustrations, opinions, and passions. Even if you are not aligned with their view or interpretation of an experience, respecting does not change your view—it allows discussion and safe space.
- Always be empathetic; don't mother or father situations.
- Forgive, forgive forgive; your job is to grow them, not judge them.
- Don't fix it, listen! Develop a space where they will leverage you to bounce concepts across without fear of your intervention.
- Reminisce with them, share memories, the history of the team, and moments, good and bad.
- They own the task—not you. Let them execute, let them make the mistake and learn. Where they do miss-step, they will learn to speak with you and seek your council.
- Promote inclusivity, down to the smallest voice from the team member with the most mundane task.
- Don't rush them in discussion, breathe—listen.
- Quality time: When they are talking—let them talk. Be fully present with them. If you are out of time, tell them and reconvene.
- Always be honest; if you cannot explain or elaborate, say so.
- Honor team traditions: meetings, celebrations, recognitions, jokes, anniversaries—the team is more important than the individual.
- Use humor—theirs, not yours. Let them breathe and find their fun in life. The world is deathly serious. Give them space to have fun.

*"Walk the talk, talk the walk, lead by example.*

## Meetings
*Get out of your team's meetings!*

Give them their mandate, boundaries, and social contract, and let them do what you are paying them to do. The only time I join team meetings is when there is any of the behavior referenced above, sandbagging, or non-collaboration, or when people are behaving like idiots, my team rarely calls on me.

My meeting structure is this: twenty-five minutes every two weeks, of which five to ten minutes is about any priority work items, and the balance is about personal topics, kids, pets, and hobbies. The alternate second week is around forty-five minutes, with the time allocation of five to ten minutes of personal talk, and the balance is around work priorities, advice, debate, frustrations, and blockers. My goal is to always be available and take any number of ad-hoc five-minute phone calls all hours of the day, night, and weekend. The recurring sessions then become intense meaningful sessions.

Recurring meetings are a waste of time and should be used as sparingly as possible. It's not the thirty or sixty minutes that is wasted—it is the time wasted from when something happens or is identified to be an issue and needs to be addressed to the time of your next recurring meeting. By being available 24/7 (they will not abuse it), you will be drawn into items in short, on-demand time slots to address whatever needs to be covered. The opportunity time savings are extraordinary.

I have found that focusing the recurring meetings on the personal side of life and deep debate/discussion and having many short, snappy, on-demand meetings has empowered my team members to be responsive and informed and to retain a sense of urgency in execution.

For the balance, make sure your team knows what is expected of them. Counsel, advise, debate the whys, and get them to execute, and then stay out of their meetings. I only join my team members' meetings when there is some form of obtuse behavior that the team members cannot course-correct by themselves. The impact of not being in team member meetings as a rule, and then being present in those exceptional meetings, is astounding.

Get out of their way while making sure they are doing what needs to be done in the most effective, relevant, and collaborative way.

### Last Words

*You are your team's servant! Lose the ego.*

Your job is to help your team members shine, so they can massively succeed in meeting their deliverables, find themselves, figure out how to work together without you being there, drive the team, and execute projects as a cohesive unit. Your job is to remove the obstacles and take the organizational hits for them. Your job is to protect them without mothering them, to quarterback situations by being the fullback. Guide them to figuring things out; don't do it for them, and do not ever claim their success as yours.

You need to decide how you want to manage or lead. In my experience, the safer you make discussion and discourse, the richer the team. You will be recognized by your leadership and the company for having a team that gets the job done. It will take time, but it will come.

*"Get busy living or get busy dying."*
—**THE SHAWSHANK REDEMPTION**

# TO BE . . . OR NOT?

This section covers a list of characteristics I believe are essential for any leader. I want you to take ownership of them in your own unique way. Embrace what feels natural, and for the parts that don't come as easily, lean on your team. Be open, be real, and ask for your team's support when you need it.

I know I'm terrible with details. Seriously, my attention to them is almost laughable, and that's okay! I'm a rock star at strategy, social and emotional awareness, quarterbacking, coaching, leading, empowering, inspiring, and enabling. If you want me to miss something, just send me a block of text. My team knows this, and they've got my back. In fact, even writing this book was a challenge! I'm sure I messed up some references, research, and URLs—the thrills of being human — but the beauty of being a leader is that you can know your strengths and weaknesses and fill in the gaps with team members who cover the areas you aren't so good at.

In this section, for each characteristic, you will find the following information:
- A definition of what I mean and personal experiences.
- A few *Ideas or Suggestions* where you can demonstrate or inspire.
- In *Authentic People*, examples of people (sports, celebrities, politicians, business leaders) in our global society that have demonstrated and lived the characteristic as well as their Wiki page.
- A few *Inspirational Videos*, most of them TED talks, where the topic is around the characteristic.
- Each section has a QR code which will link you to a web site with the embedded links.

You will notice a few persistent benefits in the characteristics, including a stronger team, team member retention, improved relationships, improved trust and credibility, a higher level of engagement, and team resilience, to name a few. Similarly, you will see repeating challenges. None of these will be in isolation, nor do you have to practice and live all of the characteristics to experience dramatically changed teams. Start somewhere, find your groove, and become the magnanimous version of yourself you want to become.

There is a companion download available with all of the URLS referenced in this book at leadingmagnanimously.com/download and includes my reading list.

You will see some Authentic People and Inspirational Videos duplicated between characteristics. I have erred on the side of repeating them so that the characteristics can be reviewed in isolation later without you flipping between pages.

There is a lot of text in this section. To help make pieces stick and to strike the emotive connection, please watch the videos. I have included a section called "Making It Real" below with reference to the specific characteristic and how I made this real. I have intentionally separated these so that when you read "Making It Real," the whole picture comes together. Feel free to bounce between the characteristics and "Making It Real" for the applicable section.

This list is intentionally alphabetical so that I do not indirectly imply those which are significant, impactful, and the most relevant in my reality onto yours.

Now, go out there and rock it! Embrace life, love your people, serve with all your heart, and let's make some magic happen together!

*So… to be… or not?*

## Be Apologetic

In my mind, being apologetic presents me as human. It tells my team that I don't have all the answers, I am an adult, and I am confident enough to admit mistakes and learn. It demonstrates vulnerability and broadcasts that I am a trusted

Apologetic

part of the team, and together we will win. It tells my team it's okay to fail, it's okay to be human.

An apologetic leader is someone who is not afraid to say, "I messed up," and take responsibility. Ownership builds trust and respect. Admitting you are wrong showcases strength and willingness to grow, creating a culture of accountability and improvement. Being apologetic involves expressing genuine regret and apology, actively listening, understanding impact, and working to make sincere efforts to fix things.

A sincere apology goes beyond "I'm sorry"; it acknowledges consequences, shows empathy, makes amends, and course corrects for any behavior that caused the situation. You connect through humility and understanding with the people you've affected and show you truly care.

Being apologetic means you are always open to learning and to making things right, a mark of professionalism and respect, helping maintain relationships.

Through apologizing, you inspire loyalty, dedication, and integrity, demonstrating that it is okay to make mistakes and you will learn from them, resulting in an engaged, cohesive, and positive environment. By doing this, you are encouraging a culture where everyone feels empowered to own up to their mistakes and collaborate on making things better.

Take the lead, show passion and your genuine heart. Show that you are being real, open, and dedicated to making a positive impact. Your team will thank you for it. A genuine apology comprises the following:

- Takes personal responsibility.
- Is totally voluntary.
- Clearly identifies what the person did wrong.
- Is condition-free.
- Clearly says, "I apologize," or, "I am sorry."
- Quickly transitions to listening.
- Includes concrete follow-up actions.
- Aligns with the accompanying gestures, facial expressions, and energy.

In *Stephen Covey's book The 7 Habits of Highly Effective People* he shares a powerful story about his son, who once said to him, "You are not sorry," after he repeatedly transgresses and apologizes. Your team will view you in the same light—and your "apology" will be irrelevant if you apologize flippantly.

Benefits you will experience by being apologetic include increased trust, enhanced credibility, and improved relationships. Your engagement will encourage accountability and facilitate learning. It will drive a significant increase in transparency, reduce fear, and boost innovation.

Some challenges you will experience include the perception of weakness and excessive vulnerability. Be careful of over-apologizing and be aware of differing cultural differences and reactions. You should be mindful in balancing humility and authority and be consistent in how, when, and why you apologize.

Some practical steps you can take to become apologetic include; quickly and authentically acknowledging mistakes, taking responsibility for whatever you did, seeking feedback, communicating transparently, and implementing changes as quickly as you can. It goes without saying that you should demonstrate that you learn from your mistakes and show empathy for those who may have been affected.

**Ideas to Demonstrate or Inspire:**
- *Mistake journals*: Of mistakes and lessons learned within the team.
- *Apology walls*: Where team members can post apologies and acknowledgments.
- *Feedback sessions*: Regular feedback sessions.
- *Anonymous apology boxes*: For reflection and learning.
- *Role-playing scenarios*: For apologizing and accepting apologies.
- *Apology workshops*: Focused on the art of apologizing and making amends.
- *Team reflection meetings*: On team mistakes and growth.
- *Recognition programs*: For team members who handle mistakes and apologies well.
- *Open forums*: For discussing mistakes and improvements.

**Authentic People:**
- Barack Obama: Frequently acknowledged mistakes and sought to correct them during his presidency.
- Kevin Rudd: Apologized on behalf of the Australian government to Indigenous Australians.
- Tiger Woods: Issued public apologies following personal scandals.
- David Beckham: Apologized for mistakes on and off the field, including a notorious red card incident.
- Howard Schultz: Apologized for Starbucks' racial bias incident and closed stores for training.

**Inspirational Voices:**
- "What I Learned from 100 Days of Rejection" by Jia Jiang. Jia shares his experience of seeking out rejection for one hundred days and the lessons he learned about resilience, humility, and the power of apologies.
- "Listening to Shame" by Brené Brown. Brené delves into the concept of shame and its impact on leadership. She explains that apologizing and owning our mistakes is crucial to overcoming shame and fostering a healthy work environment.
- "Dare to Disagree" by Margaret Heffernan. Margaret explores the value of constructive conflict and the role of apologies in leadership. She argues that leaders should embrace disagreement and be willing to apologize when wrong to foster a culture of healthy debate and innovation.
- "Our Buggy Moral Code" by Dan Ariely. Dan discusses the complexities of human morality and how people often rationalize unethical behavior. He emphasizes the importance of recognizing and apologizing for moral lapses in leadership.

## Be Authentic

For me, being authentic is always showing up as the person I am. It means my team knows at no stage is there an alternate agenda or motive to my ask, coaching, or deliverable. My team knows I care about them, and at no stage is it

Authentic

fake. By saying *always*, I mean just that, whether I am at work; in the greatest, most positive meeting or at the worst; at a social event, a conference, home, or a team event; or enjoying a personal hobby—just being authentic.

Authentic leadership is about staying true to yourself and your values. It is about being real, transparent, and ethical. It is about leveraging these principles to drive actions, rejecting conformity and masks. Standing out as a beacon of integrity and sincerity, you build trust through honesty, vulnerability, and reliability while creating a safe environment where people are valued.

Being authentic in the world today can be challenging, as social media and societal expectations expect a flawless image that we all know is not possible. Authenticity helps you form genuine connections and show up as your true self, resulting in deeper, more meaningful relationships. It is inevitable that you will attract like-minded people who appreciate you, naturally boosting your self-confidence and eliminating the need to compare yourself to others or seek external validation. The net result is you being comfortable in your own skin.

It also involves being vulnerable and open to criticism and acknowledging flaws and addressing them, regardless of how challenging. Authentic leaders foster trust and loyalty, inspire others to bring their whole selves to work, and promote creativity and innovation. This results in personal satisfaction and fulfillment.

Start by understanding and accepting the true you. Reflect on the values, beliefs, and experiences that shape your identity. Be honest about your strengths and weaknesses, and welcome feedback. Communicate transparently, sharing the thoughts, feelings, and reasons behind your decisions. Lead by example. Create a supportive environment around you so all can be heard and feel heard. You will inevitably create a ripple effect, inspiring others to be true to themselves.

The benefits you will experience from being authentic include increased trust and a much higher level of engagement. You will experience enhanced performance for yourself and your team, as well as better decision-making. You create a platform for sustained success.

Some challenges you will experience include feeling incredibly vulnerable and subjecting yourself to a lot of your own criticism. You will probably find it difficult to balance relationships while staying the leader. You will experience criticism and probably run into some cultural resistance. It's ok – you are just human.

Some practical steps you can take to become authentic include practicing self-awareness, developing relationships, and empowering others. Demonstrating consistent transparency, empathy, and adaptability helps create a pattern of authenticity from you. It is incredibly important that you align your actions with your words and recognize other people's efforts.

**Ideas to Demonstrate or Inspire:**
- *Personal storytelling sessions*: Host regular sessions where leaders and team members share personal stories.
- *Transparent decision-making workshops*: Conduct workshops where leaders explain the decision-making process for key company decisions.
- *Authenticity mentorship program*: Pair leaders with team members in a mentorship program.
- *Open feedback forums*: Create a safe space for team members to give and receive honest feedback.
- *Value-based recognition*: Recognize and reward team members who exemplify company values in their daily work.
- *Leader-led skill-sharing sessions*: Have leaders share their skills and knowledge in informal sessions.
- *Regular "Ask Me Anything" (AMA) sessions*: Hold AMA sessions where leaders answer any questions from the team.
- *Authentic leadership book club*: Start a book club focused on reading and discussing books about authentic leadership and personal development.

Authentic People:
- Angela Merkel: Pragmatic and steady leadership style has been characterized by her authenticity and commitment to transparency.
- Muhammed Ali: Authenticity was evident in his outspoken personality and unwavering principles.
- Mia Hamm: Genuine passion for soccer and her leadership in women's sports have made her an authentic role model.
- Indra Nooyi: Authenticity in her leadership and focus on sustainability have earned her widespread respect.
- Dwayne Johnson: Authenticity and down-to-earth personality have made him a highly relatable and admired celebrity.

Inspirational Voices:
- "How Great Leaders Inspire Action" by Simon Sinek. Simon explains the concept of the "Golden Circle" and how great leaders inspire action by starting with "why." Authentic leaders, according to Sinek, communicate their beliefs and inspire others to follow their vision.
- "The Transformative Power of Classical Music" by Benjamin Zander. Benjamin uses the power of music to demonstrate how authentic leaders can inspire and transform others by being passionate and true to their purpose.
- "Everyday Leadership" by Drew Dudley. Drew highlights the importance of everyday acts of leadership and how authenticity can make a significant impact in ordinary moments. He encourages leaders to recognize and celebrate their influence.

## Be Available

For me, being available means my team knows that no matter what the problem is, I am available, whenever they need me. I find the random five-minute "emergency" calls—which are not emergencies—help the team find their feet and know they can take risks and press into a new tomorrow.

Available

The short-turnaround discussions with new team members are always over the top, intense, and nearly invasive. This short-term pain turns into massive long-term gain because the team learns immediately about the greatness and holes in their decision-making and execution. This builds incredible self-confidence.

Being available is all about being approachable, accessible, and responsive for your team, always there, ready to support, guide, and assist. It is not about "being present"; it is about being emotionally and mentally engaged, a foundation of open communication and trust.

This means being available when your team needs you, answering that call, regardless of urgency and being present in the moment in the office or not, through whatever communication tools you use. Your presence includes actively listening, understanding, and empathizing with whatever the team believes needs to be brought to your attention—personal and professional. You need to be the rock your team can lean on, always supporting, encouraging, and helping with needed resources.

For you, time management and prioritization are crucial. Setting specific times aside for one-on-one meetings while being flexible with your schedule and being immediately responsive, whether face-to-face, in email, or in messaging, shows you value your team's time and concerns. This immediacy is critical—both when you are teaching them how to be autonomous and when they have got it down and need your attention.

This cultivates a sense of security and support within your team, knowing they can count on you. It also boosts job satisfaction, morale, and cohesion. The benefit of this to you is you stay in the loop about their challenges and successes, providing real-time, ongoing coaching. The culture within your team will be a great atmosphere of feeling heard, seen, and valued.

You will end up creating a supportive and trusting environment, show you care, be there when it counts, and help your team and team members thrive.

Benefits you will experience from being available include a drastic increase in team morale and communication. This will drive into increased trust and a higher level of team-member engagement. Your whole team will benefit from better, faster, richer problem-solving.

Some challenges you will experience include managing your time and avoiding burnout. It will also be difficult to keep work and personal life segmented so that you are not "always on". You will find setting boundaries to be difficult, especially as your team members enter a different level of relationship with you. You will need to tightly manage the expectations of team members who become codependent on you always being there.

Some practical steps you can take in being available include keeping your team in the loop on the general way you run your social world and personal life. Frequently challenge the team by going away for a week and having them handle the week without unnecessarily contacting you. When your team contacts you, be empathetically present and listen actively. Listen for fear, hesitation, and overconfidence. Leverage as many or as few channels for the team to get hold of you as you need, so their engagement with you doesn't draw you into all the other work.

### Ideas to Demonstrate or Inspire:

- *Virtual coffee chats*: Schedule informal virtual coffee sessions where team members can drop in for casual conversations.
- *Mobile office days*: Work from different locations within the office each week to increase visibility and accessibility.
- *"Ask Me Anything" sessions*: Hold regular AMA sessions where team members can ask questions about the company, projects, or insights.
- *Innovation hours*: Dedicate time each week for brainstorming sessions where team members can pitch new ideas.
- *Open feedback forums*: Create a monthly forum for open feedback.
- *Daily stand-ups*: Implement short daily stand-up meetings to touch base with the team and discuss priorities and concerns.
- *Mentorship circles*: Organize small mentorship circles where leaders rotate participation.

**Authentic People:**
1. Jacinda Ardern: New Zealand's prime minister is recognized for her empathetic and accessible leadership style.
2. Winston Churchill: His availability and resilience during WWII provided strong leadership for the UK.
3. Michael Jordan: Known for his leadership on and off the court, Jordan was always accessible to his teammates.
4. LeBron James: His pen communication and support for his teammates is well-recognized.
5. Dwayne Johnson: Known for his accessibility and positive interactions with fans and colleagues.

**Inspirational Voices:**
- "Why Good Leaders Make You Feel Safe" By Simon Sinek: Simon explains that great leaders create environments where people feel safe, allowing them to focus on their work rather than on protecting themselves from each other. He discusses the importance of leaders being available and approachable, fostering trust and collaboration within the team. By prioritizing the well-being of their team members, leaders can inspire loyalty and productivity.
- "How Great Leaders Inspire Action" by Simon Sinek: Simon introduces the concept of the "Golden Circle" and explains how great leaders inspire action by starting with "why." He emphasizes the importance of being available to communicate their vision and purpose clearly, which motivates and inspires their teams. Availability and clear communication are key to effective leadership.
- "The Puzzle of Motivation" by Dan Pink: Dan explores the science of motivation, highlighting the gap between what science knows and what business does. He suggests that leaders who are available and supportive of their team members' intrinsic motivations can foster a more productive and engaged workforce. Autonomy, mastery, and purpose are crucial elements that leaders should nurture.

## Be Aware

Being aware, for me, is about being in-tune with my team. Like with a radio station, the full signal needs to be in focus for you to hear everything. I work hard to be aware of the smiles, laughs, eyebrows, frowns, hands, eye contact, tone of voice, jokes, engagement style, words used, camera on or off, and sharing of tea or coffee time. Being aware helps me ensure I use the right tone and words with my team members. My goal is to ensure I know when they are being under-utilized or oversubscribed—when they are in love with their work or hating on it or team members. This awareness is reciprocated with love. My team absolutely appreciates being noticed.

Aware

Being "aware" is akin to being in tune with the pulse and heartbeat of yourself, your team, and your environment. You understand and know your strengths and weaknesses, recognize the emotions and needs of team members, and comprehend company and industry dynamics. You will be naturally perceptive, empathetic, and in sync with the ebb and flow of decision-making and relationships. It involves being conscious of your surroundings, actions, and impact on those around you, direct and indirect and practicing mindfulness in behavior, words, and attitudes.

Understanding team members deeply and knowing their strengths, weaknesses, and working styles is crucial. You need to actively listen to and observe how they communicate, collaborate, and solve problems with one another. Recognize the myriad of unique backgrounds, experiences, and perspectives.

Knowing each team member's strengths, you are able to delegate more efficiently. You will be in touch with spoken and unspoken nuances and be able to navigate toward a productive and harmonious team all while embracing diverse viewpoints and ideas that bring novel, innovative solutions and fresh approaches to projects.

You need to stay informed about current events and issues impacting your team and your company and share your awareness with the team. This includes social, political, and industry developments. Understanding the larger context in which your work takes place helps with informed decisions.

Maintaining awareness across this spectrum requires continuous and deliberate effort from you. The benefits to you are that you will create a positive and productive work environment, enhance communication, build trust, and facilitate collaboration. You will be better equipped to inspire and motivate your team, drive improved engagement and performance, and be adaptable and prepared to navigate complex unexpected situations.

Benefits you will experience by being aware include incredible changes in team dynamics and inter-team-member social awareness. You will inspire greater resilience for yourself and the team members. You will observe improved decision-making and an increase in innovation.

Some challenges you will experience include the emotional labor as you become aware of the moving emotive dynamics of your team. Being aware of people can be tiring, especially if you have no consequential action. Your team members will experience a significant amount of vulnerability as they experience how aware you are of them. Being aware is never done. It is a long-term, persistent activity for existing and new team members.

Some practical steps you can take in demonstrating awareness include practicing mindfulness as you develop your emotional intelligence. Stay informed of the happenings of your team through open communication. Reflect regularly with your team members, ask them questions, and engage with them. Create learning feedback loops for you and the team. Extend awareness beyond the team into environmental, social, economic, technical, and business spaces.

**Ideas to Demonstrate or Inspire:**
- *Mindfulness workshops*: Offer workshops on mindfulness, stress management, and emotional intelligence.
- *Environmental challenges*: Organize challenges focused on sustainability and environmental consciousness.
- *Awareness newsletters*: Create a monthly newsletter that highlights awareness topics such as mental health, diversity, and environmental issues.

- *Guest speakers and panels*: Invite guest speakers or host panels on various awareness topics.
- *Book and film club*: Start a book or film club focusing on works that promote awareness and understanding of different perspectives.
- *Awareness workshops*: Conduct workshops that focus on developing self-awareness and understanding others.
- *Team volunteering*: Organize volunteering opportunities that align with the team's values and interests.

Authentic People:
- Abraham Lincoln: Demonstrated self-awareness and empathy during the Civil War.
- Tom Brady: Known for his strategic awareness and leadership in football.
- Steve Jobs: Known for his awareness of market trends and consumer needs.
- Leonardo DiCaprio: Advocates for environmental awareness.
- Angelina Jolie: Advocates for human rights and awareness of global issues.

Inspirational Voices:
- "Your Body Language May Shape Who You Are" by Amy Cuddy: Amy discusses how body language affects how others see us and how we see ourselves. She emphasizes the importance of non-verbal cues in leadership and how being aware of our body language can enhance confidence and presence.
- "What Makes a Good Life? Lessons from the Longest Study on Happiness" by Robert Waldinger: Robert shares insights from a seventy-five-year study on happiness, highlighting the importance of relationships and social awareness in leading a fulfilling life.
- "The Power of Introverts" by Susan Cain: Susan discusses the strengths of introverts and the need for leaders to be aware of dif-

ferent personality types. She advocates for environments that allow introverts to thrive.
- "How to Make Stress Your Friend" by Kelly McGonigal: Kelly talks about the power of rethinking stress and how awareness of our responses can transform stress into a positive force.

## Be Brave

Brave

For me, being brave is putting myself out there, at risk to myself, and for the benefit and service of those around me. It means being selfless and exposing myself to situations that are incredibly exposing, potentially harmful, and risky. It is the antithesis of what a lot of people choose through being willfully blind. It is knowing that sometimes you have to take chances and demonstrate to the team that sometimes you win, and sometimes you fail. We talk about both, which inspires them to be brave, to take on tasks and responsibilities that by all accounts they would have avoided before.

Being brave is having the guts to face challenges head-on, make tough decisions, and stand firm on principles. You own your actions, act with integrity, and tackle uncertainty. You inspire and motivate others into an ongoing journey of building trust and resilience.

Step out of your comfort zone, try new things, and be willing to take risks. Embrace feedback, own mistakes, and push forward. Being brave is about innovation and experimentation; set aside time to brainstorm with and without your team. Support them through the realization of their ideas, and then celebrate with them.

Being brave also means seeking out different perspectives, welcoming and embracing new and different ways of thinking, and challenging the status quo. Transparency and honesty are key parts of bravery, having tough conversations, being open about challenges—including your own—and actively seeking out feedback.

Bravery is crucial in the creation of resilience in a dynamic environment, navigating crises and uncertainties, and making decisions that will benefit the company in the long run. You will inspire trust and confidence, encourage innovation, and cultivate an environment where everyone feels safe to express ideas. Most important is staying the course when it is tough.

You will create a resilient and innovative work environment, inspiring trust and confidence, encouraging creativity, and cultivating safety. Be brave. Embrace the challenges, and ignite creativity.

Benefits you will experience by being brave include changing the foundation on which trust in built in your team, especially when linked with authenticity. You will create a platform for dynamic team morale and resilience, a desire to be better. You will cement stronger relations with your team and change some of the dynamics of how decisions and recommendations are made.

Some challenges you will experience include risk of failure and reputational damage. You may even get yourself into a spot where physical violence may need to be avoided. Being brave will bring an inevitable flood of stress on you as you lean in, making you incredibly vulnerable. Having the team to lean on will be helpful for you.

Some practical steps you can take to become brave include self-reflection while continuously learning, standing up for decisions or team members, and exposing yourself to areas of the company others are too scared to go near. Being brave is not being dramatic. It is about facing things that are not normally faced, taking on difficult topics, and not hiding. It is about holding people to their word and social contracts, learning a new skill, challenging your or other people's foundations with the intent of creating a magnanimous tomorrow.

### Ideas to Demonstrate or Inspire:
- *Organize a "fail forward" session*: Encourage team members to share their failures and what they learned.
- *Lead an innovation challenge*: Host a competition for the best innovative ideas.

- *Have an open-door policy*: Create an environment where team members feel safe to voice their concerns.
- *Celebrate risks taken*: Recognize and reward team members who take calculated risks.
- *Host courage workshops*: Provide training on developing personal and professional bravery.
- *Be transparent with communication*: Regularly update the team on challenges and successes.
- *Encourage diversity of thought*: Promote an inclusive environment where different perspectives are valued.

**Authentic People:**
- Nelson Mandela: Fought against apartheid in South Africa and became its first black president.
- Mahatma Gandhi: Led India to independence through nonviolent resistance.
- Jesse Owens: Won four gold medals at the 1936 Berlin Olympics, challenging Nazi ideology.
- Angelina Jolie: Humanitarian efforts and advocacy for refugees.
- Keanu Reeves: Known for his humility and generosity despite immense success.

**Inspirational Voices:**
- "What it takes to be a great leader" by Roselinde Torres: Roselinde shares insights from her research on leadership, highlighting that great leaders are brave enough to anticipate the future, make courageous decisions, and build diverse networks.
- "Grit: The Power of Passion and Perseverance" by Angela Lee Duckworth: Angela discusses the role of grit in achieving success, highlighting that brave leaders persevere through challenges and inspire their teams to do the same.
- "The Courage to Tell a Hidden Story" by Eman Mohammed: Despite significant personal risks, Mohammed's work challenges stereotypes

and highlights the critical role of women in conflict zones, demonstrating the importance of bravery and determination in bringing hidden stories to light.
- "Listening to Shame" by Brené Brown: Brené explores the impact of shame on personal and professional life, urging leaders to be brave enough to confront and address shame, leading to greater authenticity and connection.

## Be Clear

For me, being clear is making sure I am heard. As you have likely noticed in this book, I speak in stories, and that does not always go down as expected. I have a bad habit of repeating myself—which I do without knowing it—until I get some form of recognition from the receiving party that they have heard me. My team has learned to engage and ask probing questions, and in doing so, they reduce the number of repeats. We often jest about it, as most often the team allows me to repeat myself. If I am not being clear, my team will challenge me, which always results in incredibly powerful, rich, insightful discussions.

Clear

Being clear ensures your team comprehends your, the team's, and the company's goals and understand expectations and roles. The intent is to leave no room for misunderstandings or confusion. This requires straightforward instruction and feedback that is easily grasped. Your decisions need to be well-defined and easy to follow.

It is about illuminating your messages and making sure they resonate with the people around you. This is achieved by using simple, concise language, removing any fluff or room for confusion. Set clear goals, deadlines, roles, and responsibilities to keep everyone aligned toward the objectives.

Embrace diverse perspectives and remain open to different, varying, conflicting viewpoints. You will need to genuinely listen and respect thoughts and opinions. By doing this, you will create lively, inclusive, and dynamic conversations, each of which is vital in maintaining vibrant communications.

You will foster trust and respect within your team. Everyone will understand what is expected along with the rationale behind decisions. Clarity reduces stress and anxiety associated with ambiguity. You will end up navigating challenges and conflicts with ease while keeping your team focused and aligned. Make every moment count, communicate with brilliance.

Benefits you will experience by being clear include improved communications and increased efficiency. You will experience higher self and team morale and better decision-making and execution. You will also develop trust in meaning what you say and doing what you say you are going to.

Some challenges you will experience include maintaining consistency and overcoming inevitable miscommunication. You will also need to balance transparency and confidentiality, finding the right time and place while handling resistance.

Some practical steps you can take to become clear include developing and enhancing your active listening and communication skills; setting clear goals and expectations with your team through open, transparent, engaging meetings; and being open to and encouraging questions and constructive feedback in the use of words, visual cue cards, and snippets of information.

**Ideas to Demonstrate or Inspire:**
- *Monthly Q&A sessions*: Host open Q&A sessions to address team concerns and provide clarity.
- *Transparent goal setting*: Collaboratively set and review goals with the team.
- *Open-door policy*: Encourage team members to approach you with questions or concerns.
- *Feedback Fridays*: Dedicate a day for providing and receiving feedback.
- *Clear onboarding process*: Develop a comprehensive and clear onboarding process for new hires.
- *Visual project boards*: Use project-management tools with clear visual boards.

- *Clarity workshops*: Conduct workshops focused on improving communication and clarity.
- *Regular check-ins*: Schedule regular one-on-one meetings to ensure clarity.
- *Clarity in email*: Send weekly summary emails highlighting key points and progress.

**Authentic People:**
- Winston Churchill: His speeches during WWII were clear and inspiring, rallying the British people during difficult times.
- Muhammad Ali: Known for his clear and bold communication style.
- Peyton Manning: Clear in his play strategies and leadership on the field.
- Jeff Bezos: Clear in his vision for Amazon and its long-term goals.
- Will Smith: Known for his clear and motivational communication style.

**Inspirational Voices:**
- "Listen, Learn . . . Then Lead" by Stanley McChrystal: General McChrystal shares lessons from his military career, emphasizing the importance of clear and adaptable leadership in complex environments.
- "Why We Have Too Few Women Leaders" by Sheryl Sandberg: Sheryl discusses the barriers women face in leadership and advocates for clear strategies to support and advance women in leadership roles.
- "The Tribes We Lead" by Seth Godin: Seth explains how clear communication and a shared vision can create powerful movements and inspire change.
- "How to Start a Movement" by Derek Sivers: Derek uses a humorous example to illustrate how clear leadership and the courage to stand out can spark a movement.

## Be Confident

For me, being confident is knowing when I know my stuff and knowing when I don't. It is about asking questions to inform myself and taking a stance on things. It is about trusting the framework and team around me, knowing that where I cannot or don't know, one of them will, and where they don't, we, the collective, will go find out and get it done.

Confident

It is being confident with and in front of my team, peers, and leaders on topics covering myself, my team, and their hobbies, world knowledge, and experience. I have learned it is okay to be confident, find out you are wrong or need to learn, and start the next morning confident as heck again.

When you are confident, every judgment and decision resonates with certainty. Being confident is believing in yourself, which inspires trust in people around you. Your actions will light up your team, creating mutual respect and empowerment, ready to conquer challenges together, fueled by a positive and unstoppable spirit.

It is all about owning your abilities and diving headfirst into challenges, having a zest for life where your energy and effective communication shine. Whether you are in meetings, tackling projects, or making decisions, it's infectious and magnetic.

You will excel at leading and inspiring those around you motivating team members to take risks and try new things. This energy drives growth and pushes boundaries. Confidence is not about arrogance. Confidence presents as healthy self-esteem, being open to feedback, ideas, and approaches. You're humble enough to admit mistakes and learn, a perfect blend of self-assuredness and openness.

You step up, taking on new responsibilities and ideas without hesitation. You handle tough situations with grace, building trust, credibility, and reliability with your team, peers, and leaders. Your job satisfaction is bound to soar, and your respect and appreciation for the diverse viewpoints and values of others will change.

Team members generally wrestle with being assertive and/or self-doubt. Confidence can be nurtured in everyone! It is like logic—once one sees it can prevail, it will. Confidence facilitates daring decisions and calculated risks, building trust and credibility. You will inspire, motivate, drive, empower, support, and create a culture of innovation and improvement.

Benefits you will experience by being confident include the spoken and unspoken trust and credibility you inherit. Your decisiveness will be an inspiration to those around you. Your change in resilience to glass half full and drive toward innovation will be remarkable.

Some challenges you will experience include inevitable overconfidence, which could be experienced as arrogance—real or perception is irrelevant You should be mindful and carefully balance the line of absolute and ongoing confidence with arrogance. You will face risks in the stances you take and will need to balance resistance with humility.

Some practical steps you can take to become confident include being incredibly self-aware, being open to learning, and ensuring you have strong mentorship around you. Your communication strategy should be to be clear and decisive and seek out feedback. While being confident, be absolutely attuned to the moving society around you, ensuring you do not cast a perceived immovable foundation around you. Encourage innovation and delegate wisely. Take responsibility and accountability for your stances, and own your outcomes.

**Ideas to Demonstrate or Inspire:**
- *Public speaking workshops*: Organize sessions to improve public speaking skills.
- *Feedback forums*: Regularly hold open forums for feedback and discussions.
- *Leadership mentoring programs*: Pair team members with confident leaders for mentorship.
- *Risk-taking challenges*: Encourage taking calculated risks on projects.
- *Team-building activities*: Foster confidence through team-building exercises.

- *Innovation days*: Allocate time for team members to work on innovative ideas.
- *Recognition programs*: Regularly recognize and celebrate achievements.
- *Leadership training*: Provide training focused on building confidence and leadership skills.
- *Role-playing scenarios*: Use role-playing to practice handling challenging situations.

**Authentic People:**
- John F. Kennedy: Confidence during the Cuban Missile Crisis.
- Michael Jordan: Confidence on and off the basketball court.
- Cristiano Ronaldo: Confident footballer with numerous accolades.
- Simone Biles: Gymnast known for her confident performances.
- Elon Musk: Confident visionary behind Tesla and SpaceX.

**Inspirational Voices:**
- "Your body language may shape who you are" by Amy Cuddy: Amy Cuddy discusses how body language affects how others see us and how we see ourselves. She explores the power of "power posing" and its impact on confidence and success.
- "Why Good Leaders Make You Feel Safe" by Simon Sinek: Simon Sinek explores how leaders who make their teams feel safe create environments where confidence and trust flourish.
- "How to Speak So That People Want to Listen" by Julian Treasure: Julian Treasure offers practical advice on speaking confidently to ensure your message is heard and respected.

## Be Consistent

For me, being consistent means showing up in a repeatable way that my team can expect. It means reacting in the same way every time regardless of the situation. It means deciding the same way every time, being persistent and pre-

Consistent

dictable. It is asking for work, paying an interest, being available, assigning work, and managing the same way every time, all the time, for each unique person.

Consistency is staying true to a set of principles and values no matter what life throws at you. Your actions match your words. Your team experiences stability and clarity. They experience someone who has got their back through thick and thin.

You need to hold onto your core values and principles, walk the talk no matter the chaos around you. It is not about being rigid; it's maintaining a steady groove that can be counted on. Keep your promises and follow through. Be dependable and true to yourself and those around you, demonstrating your consistency is the heartbeat of you. You are fully present, delivering quality work, meeting deadlines, and treating everyone with equal respect with a uniform approach to everything you do, including your words, actions, opinions, and policies.

Consistency builds trust and credibility with your team. They will know what to expect from you, knowing there are no surprises. Your behavior will facilitate effective planning, executing tasks, transparency, ideation, creativity, and problem reporting; the list is endless.

Consistency has its challenges. While it means sticking to your principles in exciting moments and the normal course of the day, it also means sticking to your principles when you are experiencing the darkest lows. This includes heated arguments, sensitive personal moments, tough decisions, reprimands, terminations, and policy enforcement—both privately and publicly.

Step into your role with passion and love, and embrace the journey. You will end up aligning a lot of people and creating a healthy, stable environment where humans flourish.

Benefits you will experience by being consistent include creating a sense of trust and reliability; people don't need to be worried about how you will show up each day. You create clarity and focus, which enhances general morale and develops stronger inter-team relationships. You facilitate better decision-making and reduce confusion and apprehension.

Some challenges you will experience include perceived non-pliability or rigidity, lack of innovation, and ideation. Time could become your enemy in being too consistent, and you may miss expectations when something goes bang in the night and you react in a way that is in significant conflict with the patterns you have set, catching people completely off-guard.

Some practical steps you can take to become consistent include defining core values and expectations by being transparent and disciplined in your approach, actions, and words. Continuously reflect and adapt while talking about this with your team. Be patient and allow your team to embrace any changes you introduce. Be sure to always be fair and follow through as you mold your consistency.

**Ideas to Demonstrate or Inspire:**
- *Daily stand-ups*: Hold brief daily meetings to align the team.
- *Weekly newsletters*: Send out regular updates on company progress and goals.
- *Consistency awards*: Recognize team members who exemplify consistency.
- *Mentorship programs*: Pair consistent leaders with new team members.
- *Clear documentation*: Maintain detailed and accessible process documentation.
- *Regular training*: Provide ongoing training and development opportunities.
- *Feedback systems*: Implement systems for regular feedback and improvement.
- *Open-door policy*: Maintain an open-door policy for transparent communication.

**Authentic People:**
- Mahatma Gandhi: Consistent in his non-violent approach to freedom.
- Winston Churchill: Known for his steadfast leadership during WWII.
- Lionel Messi: Known for his consistent excellence in soccer.

- Roger Federer: Maintained top performance in tennis.
- Taylor Swift: Known for her consistent success in music.

**Inspirational Voices:**
- "5 Ways to Lead in an Era of Constant Change" by Jim Hemerling: Jim discusses how leaders can consistently lead through change with a people-first approach.
- "The Power of Believing That You Can Improve" by Carol Dweck: Carol explains the importance of a growth mindset and consistent belief in improvement.
- "Why the Secret to Success Is Setting the Right Goals" by John Doerr: John highlights the importance of consistently setting and pursuing the right goals for success.
- "How to Manage for Collective Creativity" by Linda Hill: Linda discusses how leaders can consistently foster an environment of collective creativity.

## Be Deliberate

For me, being deliberate means my team knows there is nothing I do just to do, to brag, to keep busy, to make noise, or to take notoriety. They know that anything I ask for has purpose and intent behind it. They know they can ask me why and for what I am asking them to do something. They know I will not indulge willful blindness, self-absolution, or ignorance.

Deliberate

They know when I create urgency, it is just that, and when I chase calmness, it is just that—and everything in between. Being deliberate creates its own problems, especially in meetings, because when I am there, the entire room knows it is for a specific purpose. I hold my team and others accountable for being deliberate and intentional in what they do.

Being deliberate is about making intentional and purposeful choices, performing actions infused with meaning and precision, knowing that every step and decision will ripple through your team. You are not reacting; you are the architect of your destiny. This includes careful consideration of all angles and potential outcomes before you take action.

The art of being truly mindful, taking time to breathe, think things through, weigh the pros and cons, and move forward with clarity and confidence is deliberate. This is done through setting specific goals and objectives and charting a course to achieve them knowing your strengths and areas for growth; choices are informed and wise.

You set clear, inspiring goals and objectives and communicate openly and effectively, bringing everyone onto the same page. You seek out feedback and input because you know a variety of perspectives makes decision-making stronger. This means being proactive and taking charge; reacting is not part of your normal day.

When you're a great listener, considerate, thoughtful, responsive, and intentional, you demonstrate being deliberate. Your words are aligned and create harmony. It can be tempting, in today's whirlwind of life, to make decisions on the fly. Being deliberate requires you to slow down. It's a powerful skill that leaders need both personally and professionally.

Aspiring to be deliberate is like unlocking a superpower, it will enhance your effectiveness and credibility in a business world that's often unpredictable, fast-paced, and out of control, delivering well-informed decisions that align with your strategic vision. Make your actions count, decisions thoughtful, and leadership style and presence inspiring; be deliberate.

Benefits you will experience by being deliberate include improved and quicker decision-making, with clear ties to organizational strategy. You will experience better team alignment and sustainable growth.

Some challenges you will experience can be time consuming while causing you to be excluded from sessions where your deliberate nature and approach cause exposure for those wishing not to create visibility on progress and delivery. You need to fight your resistance to change and manage your own expectations and levels of involvement. You will need to focus on balancing flexibility and deliberation.

Some practical steps you can take to become deliberate include intense self-reflection and honest discussions with yourself. Set clear goals for yourself and your team. You should ensure you gather copious amounts of information and continuously consider alternatives, by yourself and with others. You will need to practice patience and rapidly learn from mistakes while driving intense self-reflective problem-solving.

Ideas to Demonstrate or Inspire:
- *Implement decision-making workshops*: Train team members on how to make deliberate decisions.
- *Create a feedback loop*: Encourage regular, structured feedback to improve processes.
- *Host strategy sessions*: Regularly plan and review strategic goals with your team.
- *Encourage reflective practices*: Promote journaling or reflection sessions after projects.
- *Develop a decision-making framework*: Standardize a process for making important decisions.
- *Incorporate risk assessments*: Regularly evaluate potential risks in projects and decisions.
- *Foster open communication*: Ensure everyone understands the reasoning behind decisions.

Authentic People:
- Margaret Thatcher: Known for her deliberate and decisive leadership style.
- Kobe Bryant: Renowned for his work ethic and deliberate practice routines.
- Cristiano Ronaldo: Demonstrates a deliberate approach to training and performance.
- Warren Buffett: Known for his deliberate investment strategies.
- Reese Witherspoon: Demonstrates deliberate choices in her acting and production career.

**Inspirational Voices:**
- "Why Aren't We More Compassionate?" by Daniel Goleman: Goleman discusses the deliberate practice of empathy and emotional intelligence in leadership.
- "Every Kid Needs a Champion" by Rita Pierson: Pierson talks about the deliberate effort required to connect with and inspire students, applicable to leadership in any field.
- "The Power of Believing That You Can Improve" by Carol Dweck: Dweck emphasizes the deliberate cultivation of a growth mindset for personal and professional development.
- "How to Start a Movement" by Derek Sivers: Sivers highlights the deliberate steps involved in initiating and sustaining a movement, applicable to leadership.

### Be Empathetic

For me, being empathetic is always, always putting myself in the shoes of the person I am working with or receiving a message from, especially when the message is not good news. I work hard to experience what the person will feel before I engage, and then while I am engaging. I continuously seek to know what that person is going through so that when I engage, I am constructive, considerate, and informed and have a sense of that person at that point in time. This is an emotive overload, yet the value, love and appreciation I experience as a result is overwhelming.

Empathetic

When you are empathetic, you drive the energy. You light up the room, drawing people in and making everyone feel like they belong. You truly get your team. You listen with heart. You infect those around you with warmth and feeling. You make sure everyone feels seen and heard at a personal level.

You prioritize the emotional and mental well-being of your team and others around you. You build a supportive and nurturing environment where trust and respect are foundational. You are approachable and compassionate. You go out of your way to lift people up.

Empathy is your superpower. You are tuned into the emotions of your team and others, you are an amazing listener who truly hears what others are saying, and you respond with intense kindness, appreciation, love, and understanding. You can picture yourself stepping into someone else's shoes and feeling what they feel, and you show up for them as immensely supportive and compassionate.

You actively listen and make personal connections, building a relationship on trust while you get to know your team. You continuously demonstrate you genuinely care and are aware of their emotions and reactions. You respond with a kind of kindness that makes people feel valued and appreciated.

You are a role model your team looks up to, and you lead by example. You demonstrate empathy and understanding in all decisions. You are transparent, communicate openly and clearly, and foster trust and respect. Empathy is a natural driving force behind your collaboration, what helps your team work like a well-oiled machine.

You create a positive and inclusive work environment. You listen actively and show genuine interest and concern. You are aware of your own biases and strive to keep learning from others. You cultivate a workplace culture that's buzzing with positivity.

Your energy, passion, care, and love for people make you uniquely equipped to be the driving force behind reduced stress, improved morale, and an overall boost in performance.

Benefits you will experience by being empathetic include being a massively highly respected and appreciated team member. You will dramatically impact the loyalty and retention of your team and enhance overall communication. You will create a stronger, more cohesive team that is much more resilient to conflict and strives for shared resolution.

Some challenges you will experience include a rather large emotional burden, and you will need to compartmentalize team-member experiences from the reality of your life. Maintaining objectivity will be hard, and you will need to guard yourself from over-involvement in personal and professional challenges your team members are experiencing. This strength of insight may be perceived as a weakness, but stay the course and manage time consumption. Empathetic caring and engagement will eat the clock quickly.

Some practical steps you can take to become empathetic include practicing active listening, self-awareness, and awareness of how you impact your team and they impact one another. Be mentally and emotionally present when your team engages, listening for the non-work queues. Be consistently present, learning, and teaching yourself how to deal with conflict. You will need to develop patience and the way you demonstrate appreciation for people being present and being human. Small things are the treasure chest here.

Ideas to Demonstrate or Inspire:
- *Empathy workshops*: Conduct workshops to train team members on empathetic communication and listening.
- *Peer support groups*: Create groups where team members can share experiences and support each other.
- *Anonymous feedback channels*: Provide a platform for team members to share concerns anonymously.
- *Mentorship programs*: Pair team members with mentors for personal and professional development.
- *Community service initiatives*: Organize volunteer opportunities for team bonding and empathy building.
- *Regular check-ins*: Schedule regular one-on-one meetings to understand and address team members' concerns.
- *Recognition programs*: Acknowledge and reward empathetic behaviors and teamwork.

Authentic People:
- Billie Jean King: Fought for gender equality and LGBTQ+ rights in sports.
- Magic Johnson: Raised awareness about HIV/AIDS with empathy and openness.
- Arianna Huffington: Promoted well-being and mental health in the workplace.

- Marc Benioff: Prioritized social responsibility and team member welfare at Salesforce.
- Yvon Chouinard: Promoted environmental responsibility and empathy at Patagonia.

Inspirational Voices:
- "The Danger of a Single Story" by Chimamanda Ngozi Adichie: Chimamanda highlights the importance of empathy in understanding different perspectives and avoiding stereotypes. Her talk emphasizes the need for leaders to embrace diversity and inclusivity.
- "Looking Past Limits" by Caroline Casey: Caroline shares her personal story to illustrate the power of empathy and understanding in overcoming challenges and achieving success.
- "The Danger of Silence" by Clint Smith: Clint emphasizes the importance of speaking out and empathizing with others' experiences to foster a culture of understanding and support.

## Be Fair

For me, being fair is treating people the same, all the time, on all topics. It is within equal love and appreciation that I make individual exceptions to the norm so that the sum of exceptions are fair, balanced, and aligned with the rules. It gets very hard when faced with individual trauma and life. It becomes rather clinical when you have idiots who pretend to be in it for the company, yet all they do is tacitly abuse people and policies around them.

Fair

Out of all the characteristics, this is the hardest, because being fair with rules and decisions between people means some people unintentionally gain advantage and some are negatively impacted; some you want to help more, however in doing so I would create an imbalance on the persistent execution of rule. This is hard for me.

Being fair is about treating all team members with equal love and respect, making decisions based on what's right and just, steering clear of favoritism. You create an environment where trust and respect grow like wildflowers.

You ensure all people have an equal and fair experience around being heard, paid, led, managed, trained, coached, and praised, to name a few. You work to ensure everyone is treated equally and impartially. You ensure all voices are heard. You are open-minded and explore different ideas and experiences before making a call. Fairness guides you to act with integrity and respect.

Being fair in today's beautifully diverse world means acknowledging and cherishing the uniqueness of humanity. This extends to backgrounds, beliefs, experiences, and the sum of the people that make up your team. It's about recognizing and understanding that everyone's journey is different; you value everyone's story.

You actively listen to all perspectives and concerns through open communication and transparency. You strive to find that sweet spot between the needs of your team members, your team, and the company. Your mission is to create a harmonious work environment where everyone experiences wins.

You treat everyone without bias or discrimination, recognizing and addressing power imbalances and systemic inequalities. You value each team member's unique qualities and contributions without creating a hierarchy and strive to ensure everyone feels seen and heard.

You keep an eye on the company's goals and sometimes must make tough decisions, such as allocating resources, cutting budgets, letting someone go, or setting performance expectations.

Being fair is crucial for cultivating a positive workplace culture where team members feel valued and respected, a place where fairness fuels trust and team cohesion, where conflicts and the intensity thereof are reduced.

Benefits you will experience by being fair include the development of trust and respect within the team and wider. You will enhance productivity and create a positive reputation for yourself and the company. You will end up attracting and retaining team members.

Some challenges you will experience include the subjectivity of what "fair" means. You will be challenged in balancing individual, team, and company interests. Managing perception will be tough, as being fair with one person may be perceived as giving that person more or less what others have received. Being consistent will be tough, and managing conflict with people demanding or begging for exception will be hard.

Some practical steps you can take to become fair include doing intense self-reflection and self-assessment. You need to create clear policies and feedback mechanisms to ensure your policies are clear. Strive for ongoing insights and learning, seek equal and equitable outcomes that are consistent. Active listening and transparent decision-making are critical; only you will look yourself in the mirror tomorrow, and you will never know when the person that feels they either won larger or were mistreated will talk with someone else, resulting in a difficult set of ripple affects you need to manage.

Ideas to Demonstrate or Inspire:
- *Diversity workshops*: Organize workshops on diversity and inclusion.
- *Anonymous feedback*: Implement anonymous feedback systems to ensure all voices are heard.
- *Equal pay audits*: Conduct regular pay audits to ensure fairness.
- *Mentorship programs*: Establish mentorship programs for underrepresented groups.
- *Fair hiring practices*: Ensure unbiased recruitment processes.
- *Transparent promotion criteria*: Make promotion criteria clear and transparent.
- *Conflict mediation*: Provide training on conflict mediation and resolution.

Authentic People:
- Eleanor Roosevelt: Eleanor championed human rights and equal treatment, playing a key role in drafting the Universal Declaration of Human Rights.

- Muhammad Ali: Muhammad not only excelled in boxing but also advocated for social justice and fairness outside the ring.
- Satya Nadella: Satya promotes a culture of fairness and inclusivity at Microsoft, focusing on empowering every person and/organization.
- Sheryl Sandberg: Sheryl promotes fairness and equality at Facebook (now Meta), focusing on creating a more inclusive workplace.
- Beyoncé: Beyoncé advocates for fairness and equality through her music and philanthropy, using her influence to promote social justice causes.

Inspirational Voices:
- "What Makes Us Feel Good About Our Work?" by Dan Ariely. Dan examines how fairness in recognizing effort and achievement significantly impacts team member satisfaction and productivity.
- "How to Fix a Broken School? Lead Fearlessly, Love Hard" by Linda Cliatt-Wayman. Linda shares her experience in turning around failing schools by leading with fairness and compassion.
- "The Transformative Power of Classical Music" by Benjamin Zander. Benjamin uses the metaphor of classical music to illustrate how fair and inspiring leadership can unlock the potential in others.

## Be Gentle

For me, being gentle means knowing my words or actions can hurt and cause invisible damage. I know I need to be firm with my team and focused on company outcomes. This should not impact how I engage with my team members and the individual, socially aware respect of engagement I owe them. I know that I can be incredibly gentle while being very deliberate. In the most vulnerable of moments for my team members, I know that I win by being the gentlest human I can.

Gentle

As a gentle leader, you lead with kindness, empathy, understanding, and caring, creating vibrant and supportive spaces where everyone feels valued and heard. You actively listen and communicate with a warm heart. You are patient in your interactions, setting the stage for trust and respect. You are about lifting each other up and inspiring greatness.

You prioritize love and compassion. You build genuine, heartfelt relationships through understanding feelings and needs and treating everyone with empathy.

Your effective communication is a secret sauce. You are mindful of your words and tone and always steer clear of aggression and/or confrontation. You use uplifting and encouraging language. You care about your team's ideas and concerns, showing them they're not just team members, but rather part of a family. You set boundaries calmly and with respect. You ensure everyone knows where they stand without feeling alienated.

You balance assertiveness with empathy. You work to understand that every personality and communication style is unique, and you adapt your approach. This is being effective and considerate. You ensure harmony and productivity. You are kind and thoughtful, yet assertive and efficient.

This kind of leader brings a treasure trove of benefits, including motivation, harmony, productivity, and a calm environment. You manage conflicts through your gentle approach, leading to better resolutions and problem-solving. Embrace gentleness in your leadership style and transform the lives around you.

Benefits you will experience by being gentle include increased team member engagement and higher productivity. The team's morale will improve along with conflict resolution. You will experience an enhanced sense of trust as well

Some challenges you will experience include a perception of weakness and an inability to handle difficult team members and situations. You may experience a resistance to change and lack of available time.

Some practical steps you can take to become gentle include developing emotional intelligence and practice active listening. You should work on empathetic communications and being incredibly patient when your team members try explain situations to you. Give copious amounts of feedback and encourage collaboration. Recognize and celebrate achievement, public or private. Encourage personal and professional development and a socially accepting work environment.

**Ideas to Demonstrate or Inspire:**
- *Start a kindness initiative*: Encourage acts of kindness among team members.
- *Hold regular check-ins*: Schedule one-on-one meetings to listen and support team members.
- *Create a comfortable workspace*: Ensure the physical environment is welcoming and comfortable.
- *Offer well-being programs*: Provide resources and programs for mental and physical health.
- *Celebrate diversity*: Highlight and celebrate the diverse backgrounds of team members.
- *Provide flexible working hours*: Allow for flexibility to accommodate personal needs.
- *Encourage volunteering*: Organize volunteer opportunities for the team.
- *Recognize personal milestones*: Acknowledge and celebrate personal achievements and events.

**Authentic People:**
- Justin Trudeau: Canadian prime minister known for his focus on inclusion and empathy.
- Ellen Johnson Sirleaf: Liberia's first female president known for her compassionate leadership.
- Manny Pacquiao: Boxer known for his humility and gentle personality outside the ring.
- Sachin Tendulkar: Cricket legend known for his humility and respectful demeanor.
- Dolly Parton: Known for her philanthropy and gentle nature.
- Robin Williams: Known for his kind-hearted and gentle nature.

Inspirational Voices:
- "Take 'The Other' to Lunch" by Elizabeth Lesser: Elizabeth encourages reaching out to those with differing views and engaging in compassionate conversations to foster understanding and empathy.
- "Why Aren't We More Compassionate?" by Daniel Goleman: Daniel discusses the science behind compassion and its importance in leadership and human connections.
- "10 Ways to Have a Better Conversation" by Celeste Headlee: Celeste provides practical tips for having meaningful and empathetic conversations, essential for gentle leadership.

## Be Graceful

For me, being graceful means conducting what I do with professional eloquence. I work to be above the moment and always devote and extreme sense of respect and appreciation for the team member. I work hard to be a ballroom dancer in the middle of the work activity, working hard to help everyone be magnificent at what they do and place them on their own success pedestal, public or private.

Graceful

Being a graceful leader, while being cool under pressure, is about embodying elegance and calmness in all interactions and decisions. You navigate challenges with composure and make integrous choices underpinned by empathy and respect.

Your communication style becomes a powerful tool, where you ensure your words and actions build trust and foster collaboration. This means handling adversity with dignity and staying composed under pressure. You inevitably will inspire people around you through your serene and thoughtful demeanor.

It is about poise and tact done professionally, keeping your cool and showing respect, especially when the going gets tough.

You are mindful of words and actions. You are considerate of the impacts of people around you, handling conflict with diplomacy and avoid causing harm or offense. You adapt to change and handle unexpected situations with ease. You are an effective communicator that easily empathizes with others. You maintain a positive attitude through great and rough times. Your emotional intelligence and the management of your emotions is impressive and deliberate in your reactions.

Your team experiences a positive and productive work environment lathered in professionalism, care, empathy, and love which helps you and the team to navigate difficult situations with ease. You inspire and motivate a positive and inclusive environment. You set a positive tone by showing respect and kindness. You handle tasks with grace and efficiency, creating a culture of mutual respect and professionalism. You foster and maintain team cohesion and mutual respect.

Benefits you will experience by being gentle include enhanced team morale and increased trust—improved and more effective problem resolution along with enhanced inter-team-member and team communication. You will also experience a drastically impacted work culture.

Some challenges you will experience include maintaining your composure between a wide range of scenarios and situations. You will need to balance empathy and authority while ensuring you are not perceived as weak or frivolous. Consistency, while difficult, is important to maintain.

Some practical steps you can take to become gentle include practicing active listening and demonstrating open communication and transparency. You will need to stay composed under pressure and develop a deep sense of emotional intelligence. You will need to invest in a significant amount of personal-professional presence and growth, recognizing and appreciating contributions while remaining composed under intense pressure. Humility and humbleness is core to being gentle.

**Ideas to Demonstrate or Inspire:**
- *Gratitude board*: Create a gratitude board where team members can leave notes of appreciation for their colleagues.

- *Mindfulness sessions*: Offer regular mindfulness or meditation sessions to help team members manage stress and maintain a composed demeanor.
- *Empathy workshops*: Conduct workshops focused on building empathy and understanding among team members.
- *Conflict resolution training*: Provide training on graceful conflict resolution techniques.
- *Storytelling circles*: Organize storytelling sessions where team members can share personal experiences that highlight acts of grace and kindness.
- *Recognition programs*: Implement a formal recognition program that rewards team members who demonstrate grace and empathy in their interactions.
- *Peer support groups*: Establish peer support groups where team members can discuss challenges and offer each other guidance and encouragement.
- *Community service projects*: Organize team-building activities that involve giving back to the community.

### Authentic People:
- Queen Elizabeth II: Exemplified grace throughout her long reign.
- Mother Theresa: Though not a politician, her influence and grace in humanitarian efforts are widely recognized.
- Larry Page: Co-founded Google and led with a graceful approach to innovation.
- Audrey Hepburn: Known for her elegance and humanitarian work.

### Inspirational Voices:
- "How to Build Your Confidence—And Spark It in Others" by Brittany Packnett: Brittany emphasizes the importance of grace in building confidence and empowering others. She shares strategies for fostering a confident and supportive team environment.

- "The Secret to Great Opportunities? The Person You Haven't Met Yet" by Tanya Menon: Tanya highlights the importance of building diverse and inclusive networks with grace and openness and how these connections can lead to unexpected opportunities.
- "The Art of Asking" by Amanda Palmer: Amanda explores the grace involved in asking for help and building connections. She shares her experiences as an artist and leader, demonstrating how vulnerability and trust can foster strong, supportive communities.

### Be Human

For me, being human is just that—being human. I chose to see everyone with individual eyes, I do not bucket or profile. I work with people as they present themselves. Most desire to exceed what they could ever have dreamt to be, and others are okay with who they are, and I choose to engage as they choose to be engaged with. Life is tough as it is, and I

Human

work to get the team dynamics to a place where people love one another as they are for what they are and help fill in the blank spots. I love and accept as people are. This does not mean I am not disappointed or don't feel let down by people. I just allow people who want to be what they are to be, and for those who want to exceed, I help them drive.

Being human is diving into the beautiful mess of our human qualities. It is about embracing empathy, vulnerability, authenticity, and compassion. You create connections that matter. You light up your team's world with a sense of value and support. Your motivation and transparency are beyond measure. You are approachable and not afraid to say, "I messed up," and, "Here's how we're moving forward."

You celebrate our humanity. You truly see and appreciate everyone's uniqueness. You appreciate and respect perspectives and experiences. You step up with empathy and compassion. You create a vibe of inclusion and support.

You are attuned to keeping in mind that life throws us all curveballs. You are there for your team when they need it most; you show up. You radiate genuine understanding and authenticity. You are always your true self, emotions and the whole nine yards. You carry no masks or pretense. Just you, relatable.

You communicate with heart and collaborate with spirit. You face challenges and conflicts head-on, maturely and professionally.

You create a work environment that feels like home. You foster trust and loyalty. You encourage open and honest conversations and nurture mutual respect. You live out the values of compassion and integrity, embrace your humanity, lead with heart.

Benefits you will experience by being human include increased trust and loyalty from your team. You will experience higher and improved team-member engagement along with better team collaboration. You will observe an impact and change in team and influenced company culture. You will also experience a desire for enhanced problem-solving and enhanced and different outcomes.

Some challenges you will experience include balancing empathy and authority while managing vulnerability risks. You will probably feel an emotional drain and a self and team resistance to change. It is probable you will experience delays in decision-making as a result of the individual impacts.

Some practical steps you can take to become human include developing your self-awareness and active listening skills. Show vulnerability and cultivate empathy. Encourage open communications and prioritize the well-being of your team and team members.

Ideas to Demonstrate or Inspire:
- *Storytelling sessions*: Share personal stories of challenges and successes to inspire empathy and connection.
- *Gratitude wall*: Create a space where team members can post notes of appreciation for their colleagues.
- *Mental health days*: Introduce dedicated days off for team members to focus on their mental well-being.
- *Volunteer programs*: Organize team volunteering events to foster a sense of community and give back.
- *Open-door policy*: Encourage leaders to have an open-door policy for team members to discuss concerns and ideas.

- *Mindfulness workshops*: Offer sessions on mindfulness and stress management.
- *Peer recognition programs*: Implement programs where team members can recognize and reward each other's efforts.

**Authentic People:**
- Mahatma Gandhi: Led with non-violence and empathy.
- Mother Teresa: Dedicated her life to serving the poor and sick.
- LeBron James: Focused on community upliftment and education.
- Keanu Reeves: Renowned for his kindness and humility.
- Chris Evans: Advocated for political awareness and social issues.

**Inspirational Voices:**
- "The Tribes We Lead" by Seth Godin: Seth discusses how leaders create movements by connecting and leading tribes, groups of people with shared interests and goals.
- "The Art of Asking" by Amanda Palmer: Amanda talks about the power of asking for help and building connections, demonstrating vulnerability and trust in leadership.
- "How to Make Work-Life Balance Work" by Nigel Marsh: Nigel discusses the challenges of work-life balance and offers practical advice on how to achieve a healthier balance as a leader.
- "What It Takes to Be a Great Leader" by Roselinde Torres: Roselinde shares insights from her research on what makes a great leader in the modern world, emphasizing adaptability, diversity, and the ability to anticipate change.

## Be Inspirational

For me, being inspirational is just being me. I love life and people. I engage with everything, all the time. I am able to inspire from the outset with people I know and people I have just met. I have been told my energy and love for life is contagious and a breath of fresh air. I am like this because

Inspirational

I have chosen it. I have experienced some of the darkest parts of life, and I chose to live above them. I actively chose to celebrate life and love people, every moment of every day—as much as I am able to muster. You need to find your version of being inspiring; ask yourself – how do you inspire people around you, what comes naturally.

When you are inspirational, you light up the room with energy and enthusiasm. You dream of a bright future and share that dream. You make people around you feel excited and alive. You spark passion and drive in others through a compelling vision that's downright electrifying.

You are full of charisma and genuine authenticity, a beacon of trust and respect. You walk the talk and lead by example, with integrity and empathy as your foundation. You create a space where collaboration is the heartbeat of everything you do. You lift others up, empowering them, creating a hunger to reach for the stars and come up with the most creative and innovative ideas.

You are the team's cheerleader. You notice and celebrate wins, big or small. You strive for everyone to be the rock stars they are. Personal growth is key, and you invest in your team's development. You are the calm in the storm and navigating optimism with a can-do attitude. You connect on a deep human level. You are about creating a sense of purpose and belonging. Your vision is beyond a mere destination; it's a journey, something truly special.

Authenticity and integrity are at your core. You are genuine and true to your values. This builds a solid foundation of trust and credibility. You consistently demonstrate the attitudes and behaviors you want to see in your team. This fosters a culture of trust and respect.

Your secret sauce is empathy and emotional intelligence. You tune into the emotions and perspectives of your team. You connect on a level that is real and heartfelt. By showing genuine care, you create an environment where people feel valued and supported. You're self-aware, managing your own emotions effectively, which helps you stay composed and steady even when things get tough.

Empowerment is your middle name, and you are committed to your team's growth and success. You give autonomy and expect your team to make decisions and take ownership. Resilience is your superpower. You maintain a positive outlook and see challenges as opportunities. This positive mindset inspires your team through tough times. You foster a culture of optimism and perseverance.

Inspiring means creating a compelling vision, leading with authenticity and integrity. You connect with people on an emotional level. Your impact is about the lasting legacy you leave and the lives you touch and inspire. This aligns with your values of empathy, integrity, and growth, allowing you to lead authentically.

Benefits you will experience by being inspirational include enhanced team performance and higher team-member retention. You will experience increased team member collaboration and greater job satisfaction. You will also observe an improvement in organizational culture.

Some challenges you will experience include sustaining motivation and energy. You will need to balance empathy and authority while handling criticism. Managing your own energy and stress while adapting to an ever-changing environment is critical.

Some practical steps you can take to become inspirational include developing and enriching your emotional intelligence and communication effectiveness. Encourage growth, instill trust, and foster a positive culture. Share a compelling vision with your team and encourage innovation. Provide mentorship and coaching while fostering collaboration. Maintaining your energy and positive state of mind are critical.

**Ideas to Demonstrate or Inspire:**
- *Vision workshops*: Conduct interactive sessions where team members can contribute to the company's vision and goals.
- *Storytelling sessions*: Share personal and organizational success stories to motivate and inspire the team.
- *Recognition programs*: Create programs that regularly acknowledge and reward outstanding efforts and achievements.
- *Open forums*: Hold regular open forums for team members to voice their ideas and concerns, promoting transparency.

- *Mentorship programs*: Pair experienced leaders with emerging talent for mutual growth and inspiration.
- *Innovation challenges*: Organize challenges that encourage creative problem-solving and innovation.
- *Team-building retreats*: Plan retreats that focus on building relationships and fostering a shared vision.
- *Guest speakers*: Invite inspirational speakers to share their experiences and insights with the team.

Authentic People:
- Richard Branson: Founder of Virgin Group, known for his adventurous spirit and business acumen.
- Taylor Swift: Singer-songwriter, known for her advocacy for artists' rights and empowerment.
- Keanu Reeves: Actor, known for his humility and generosity, inspiring many with his down-to-earth nature.

Inspirational Voices:
- "Why We Do What We Do" by Tony Robbins: Tony explores the psychological forces that drive human behavior and how leaders can harness these forces to inspire and motivate others.
- "Grit: The Power of Passion and Perseverance" by Angela Lee Duckworth: Angela highlights the role of grit in achieving success and how leaders can foster resilience in themselves and their teams.
- "The Danger of a Single Story" by Chimamanda Ngozi Adichie: Chimamanda discusses the power of storytelling and the importance of diverse perspectives in leadership and society.
- "Are You a Giver or a Taker?" by Adam Grant: Adam examines the dynamics of giving and taking in the workplace, advocating for a culture of generosity and collaboration.
- "How Great Leaders Inspire Action" by Simon Sinek: Simon discusses the importance of the "why" in leadership, explaining how great leaders inspire action by communicating their purpose and vision

## Be Intentional

For me, being intentional is the precursor to being deliberate. I engage with intent and cause. I don't do things just to do; there is always an outcome. I sometimes have taken this too far, where my kids have challenged me on discussions and engagement, saying I don't do anything without specific intent. I work hard to balance engagement—at work, everything is with intent to maximize the team to the benefit of the company while not misusing this.

Intentional

Being intentional means making every action count, every decision purposeful. Being intentional is about embracing deliberate choices. These choices align with your values and dreams. They are the heartbeat of your team and the company. You make decisions that resonate with your core. You are crystal clear in your communication, and you stay true to your actions.

You dance to your own beat within the vision of the company, setting clear, exciting goals. You craft plans to realize them. You are normally the seed energy, being astutely aware of how you impact people around you. You are dedicated to creating a space where everyone thrives and feels the vibes.

You are deeply self-aware and strategic, constantly thinking, "How can I make this better?" "How can I lift others up?" You are driven by a passion to improve yourself and everyone around you, continuously.

You make every decision with purpose. Your actions align with your wildest dreams and most cherished values. You are mindful and full of fun in your approach to work. Every moment matters; you make every moment count. Life is not on autopilot for you. You seldom allow external factors to sway you. The driver's seat is your home.

You know your strengths and embrace your quirks. You are present in every moment, deeply engaged with your surroundings and the people in them. You listen with your heart. You attend to your needs and emotions all the time. You welcome new experiences and perspectives with open arms, always. You set clear, exciting goals for yourself and your team. You see opportunities for improvement and jump on them with a smile. You build positive, supportive relationships around you.

In our fast-paced world, being intentional is essential for personal and professional growth. It helps you stand out. It allows you to lead with purpose. You build trust and respect with those around you, and loyalty within your team. Lead with intention, passion, and a zest for life. Make every moment count.

Benefits you will experience by being intentional include an improved clarity and focus that results in enhanced trust and respect. You will experience enhanced engagement and productivity, better decision-making and increased personal fulfilment.

Some challenges you will experience include a draw on both time and effort, and your own resistance to change. You will need to balance priorities and manage through ambiguity while maintaining consistency.

Some practical steps you can take to become intentional include the development of self-awareness and effective communication. Be consistent in your engagement style and feedback while remaining adaptable. Focus on prioritizing self-care, and foster a positive culture. You should regularly communicate your vision and encourage professional development (for yourself and your team).

### Ideas to Demonstrate or Inspire:
- *Intentional goal-setting workshops*: Help team members set and align personal and professional goals.
- *Purpose-driven projects*: Assign projects that align with the company's mission and values.
- *Mindfulness sessions*: Incorporate mindfulness practices to enhance focus and intention.
- *Leadership training programs*: Develop programs focused on intentional leadership skills.
- *Regular reflection meetings*: Encourage teams to reflect on their progress and intentional actions.

- *Mentorship programs*: Pair team members with mentors to guide intentional career growth.
- *Values-based decision-making*: Implement frameworks that prioritize company values in decision-making.
- *Vision board workshops*: Encourage team members to create vision boards to visualize their goals.

## Authentic People:
- Lee Kuan Yew: Transformed Singapore into a global financial hub through strategic policies, anti-corruption measures, and investment in education and infrastructure.
- Eleanor Roosevelt: Advocated for human rights and chaired the committee for the Universal Declaration of Human Rights, reshaping global policies.
- Ronald Reagan: Implemented economic reforms and strategically engaged with the Soviet Union, contributing to the Cold War's end.
- Babe Ruth: Demonstrated focus and intentional practice, revolutionizing baseball.
- Natalie Portman: Chose strategic roles and engaged in activism for social causes.

## Inspirational Voices:
- "Why We Have Too Few Women Leaders" by Sheryl Sandberg: Sheryl addresses the barriers to women's leadership and emphasizes the need for intentional actions to support and empower women in leadership roles. She calls for conscious efforts to create inclusive and equitable workplaces.
- "The Difference Between Winning and Succeeding" by John Wooden: Legendary coach John shares his philosophy on success and leadership. He advocates for intentional focus on personal and team development rather than solely on winning, highlighting the importance of character and effort.

- "True North" by Bill George: Bill discusses the importance of authentic leadership and finding one's "true north." He emphasizes the need for intentional self-discovery and alignment with personal values to lead effectively.

## Be Interested

Interested

For me, being interested is being curious about my team, what drives them, and why. I want to know why they have chosen their profession, what they surround themselves with, what hobbies they have and why, and how they gain fulfillment from them. I also want to know who their significant others and children are and how they keep their world glued together. I pay an active interest in what they love, what gets them through the day, and what their struggles are. I am always looking to learn from and about the team, life, society, and new norms—I never stop growing and expanding my mind.

When you are interested, you thrive on genuine curiosity and vibrant engagement. You dive headfirst into your work and team. You immerse yourself into the world around you with infectious enthusiasm. While hitting targets, you are deeply invested in the journey. You savor every moment of connection and growth. You embrace a dynamic, ever-evolving process where every voice matters, every idea has a place.

You have an insatiable curiosity about people and life, bathing in experiences and soaking up knowledge like a sponge. You embrace different perspectives with an open heart and mind. When you are interested, you are fully engaged. You are constantly looking to learn more, understand more, see more, know more, do more.

You attend meetings wholeheartedly to share ideas, spark discussions, debate, and collaborate. Your presence shows your awareness of objectives and your passion for them. When new projects come your way, you jump in with both feet. You are always growing, encouraging people to grow.

Your interest extends beyond the office walls. You seek out opportunities to connect with like-minded individuals. You join clubs and attend events. You engage in online communities. You are always on the lookout for mentors and experts to learn from. This thirst for connection and knowledge keeps you vibrant and inspired.

You build relationships with coworkers and leaders. As a team player, you are always ready to lend a hand. Your actions create a ripple effect where everyone feels valued and motivated.

This brings a treasure trove of benefits. On a personal level, it fuels your growth and fulfillment. It keeps you engaged and evolving. Professionally, it transforms your team into a powerhouse of motivation and loyalty. Your genuine interest in their development creates a dynamic, productive atmosphere where everyone thrives. Embrace the journey, and let your curiosity lead the way. Be passionately interested.

Benefits you will experience by being interested include enhanced team engagement and improved innovation. You will experience better decision-making by yourself and by the team. You will develop stronger relationships and increase team member retention.

Some challenges you will experience include emotional investment and time-management impacts. You may be overwhelmed and battle with setting boundaries. You will absolutely experience skepticism.

Some practical steps you can take to become interested include the development of active listening and continuously learning. Be present in discussions, show empathy, and encourage collaboration. Provide feedback and celebrate achievements.

### Ideas to Demonstrate or Inspire:
- *Book clubs*: Start a book club to discuss relevant industry books and foster a love of learning.
- *Lunch and learn*: Host informal sessions where team members can share knowledge on various topics.
- *Team outings*: Organize team-building activities and social events to strengthen relationships.

- *Open office hours*: Set aside time for open-door discussions, allowing team members to share their ideas and concerns.
- *Personal growth plans*: Work with each team member on a personal development plan, showing interest in their growth.
- *Recognition programs*: Implement programs to regularly acknowledge and celebrate individual and team achievements.
- *Suggestion boxes*: Create a platform for team members to share their ideas and feedback anonymously.
- *Innovation challenges*: Host competitions to encourage creative problem-solving and new ideas.

Authentic People:
- Jacinda Ardern: Demonstrates a genuine interest in her country's welfare and social issues, leading with compassion and openness.
- Theodore Roosevelt: His interest in conservation led to significant environmental policies and the establishment of national parks.
- Reed Hastings: Promotes a culture of freedom and responsibility, transforming Netflix into a leading streaming service.
- George Clooney: Active in social and political causes, using his fame to raise awareness on critical issues.

Inspirational Voices:
- "The Happy Secret to Better Work" by Shawn Achor: Shawn explains how positive psychology can enhance productivity and happiness at work. Leaders who show interest in the well-being of their team create a more engaged and motivated workforce.
- "A Guide to Collaborative Leadership" by Lorna Davis: Lorna discusses the importance of collaboration and vulnerability in leadership. By being genuinely interested in building partnerships, leaders can achieve greater collective success.
- "The Difference Between Winning and Succeeding" by John Wooden: Legendary coach John shares his philosophy on success, emphasizing

personal bests over winning. Leaders who show interest in the holistic development of their team foster true success.
- "10 Ways to Have a Better Conversation" by Celeste Headlee: Celeste offers practical tips for meaningful conversations. Leaders who master these skills show genuine interest in their interactions, enhancing communication and connection.
- "Your Elusive Creative Genius" by Elizabeth Gilbert: Elizabeth shares her insights on nurturing creativity. Leaders who are interested in supporting creative efforts can inspire innovation and growth within their teams.

## Be Kind

For me, being kind is approaching everything with an open heart and mind, always keeping in mind that things can be harder and worse. I look for the best in people and always assume the best will show up. Only a few times in my life have I met the absolute worst. I engage with people with humility and reverence, always looking to draw the most human out of them.

Kind

When you are kind, you are about bringing that vibrant, human touch to your leadership style. You lead with your heart wide open. You embrace empathy, compassion, and understanding. You light up the room, everyone knows they can turn to you because you genuinely care. You are the one who sees people, really sees them. You recognize their efforts and support them when they need it most, typically in the most unexpected ways.

You create an environment where everyone feels respected and valued. Kindness is not about being soft or avoiding tough calls. You blend firmness with empathy, making decisions that honor the human experience. You ensure every action is soaked in consideration for its human impact.

You treat everyone with a big-hearted approach—compassion. You are understanding and respectful. You have a knack for tuning in to your team members' perspectives regardless of how much they differ from your own.

You make them feel heard and understood. You are considerate and thoughtful in your actions and words. Empathy and support are like confetti at a celebration. You create an environment that thrives on positivity and inclusivity.

Kindness is your superpower. You leverage it to build an inclusive work environment where everyone feels valued, heard. You are a catalyst for teamwork and collaboration. You encourage engagement of ideas without fear of judgment. Your mindful approach to communication and conflict resolution shows that you understand the profound impact your words and actions can have on others. Your approach touches everyone you interact with.

It promotes teamwork and collaboration, creating trust and camaraderie. It is a secret sauce for a healthy work-life balance. It reduces stress and boosts job satisfaction. It provides a foundation of a strong company culture. It facilitates immense productivity and retention.

Your kindness is a game-changer. You create a positive, productive work environment. You yield trust and loyalty. When you care for your team, they become more engaged. This drives motivation and commitment. This then facilitates the walk toward loyalty.

Benefits you will experience by being kind include enhanced team-member engagement and increased loyalty and team member retention. You will experience better team and inter-team collaboration along with a stronger drive toward an inclusive, more deeply caring organizational culture. You will develop a great reputation and have a great sense of personal fulfilment.

Some challenges you will experience include a perceived weakness and difficulty in balancing kindness with authority. You will end up with some difficult decisions where rule overrides being kind. You need to manage expectations and work hard to avoid burnout through going the extra mile and then some in caring for and being kind to your team.

Some practical steps you can take to become kind include practicing active listening and expressing gratitude. Show empathy and provide support along with being transparent and encouraging team-member growth. You should foster inclusivity, create mentorship programs, and demonstrate empathy in action.

### Ideas to Demonstrate or Inspire:
- *Random acts of kindness*: Encourage team members to perform random acts of kindness for each other.
- *Gratitude wall*: Create a space where team members can post notes of appreciation.
- *Kindness awards*: Recognize and reward acts of kindness within the team.
- *Volunteering opportunities*: Organize team volunteering events.
- *Wellness Wednesdays*: Implement a weekly wellness initiative.
- *Team lunches*: Host regular team lunches to foster camaraderie.
- *Peer recognition programs*: Encourage team members to acknowledge their peers' efforts.

### Authentic People:
- Dalai Lama: Spiritual leader of Tibet, advocating for peace and kindness worldwide.
- Eliud Kipchoge: Marathon runner, celebrated for his humility and work in promoting education in Kenya.
- Naomi Osaka: Tennis player, known for her activism on social justice issues and charitable contributions.
- John Legend: Singer, known for his activism on social justice issues and charitable contributions.

### Inspirational Voices:
- "Take 'The Other' to Lunch" by Elizabeth Lesser: Elizabeth encourages people to connect with others who hold different beliefs, promoting kindness and understanding.
- "The Danger of Silence" by Clint Smith: Clint discusses the importance of speaking up for justice and kindness, encouraging leaders to use their voices for good.
- "The Price of Shame" by Monica Lewinsky: Monica speaks about the power of empathy and kindness in overcoming public humiliation and fostering compassion.

- "Try Something New for 30 Days" by Matt Cutts: Matt encourages trying new things to break routines and grow, highlighting the importance of supportive and kind leadership.
- "Color Blind or Color Brave?" by Mellody Hobson: Mellody discusses the importance of being brave and open about race, advocating for kindness and inclusivity in leadership.

## Be Loved

For me, being loved is allowing myself to be loved by my team. It means exposing myself to be completely loved and appreciated by my team. That means being vulnerable and accessible to them.

Loved

When you are loved, you allow yourself to be loved; you need to allow yourself to be loved. You celebrate with your team in love. You lead with your heart wide open. You embrace every moment with empathy and kindness. Your heart screams authenticity. You create a vibrant, inclusive environment. Your team members feel valued and respected. You surround yourself with a buzz and inspiration.

You make everyone's well-being and growth a top priority. You show real care for their journeys. You care about both their personal and professional worlds. You build trust by being transparent. You listen with your whole being. You align your actions with your words. Your team knows they can come to you with anything.

You are not afraid to admit when you're wrong. You are always up for learning and growing alongside your team. You celebrate successes together. When things go south, you are there, turning the experience into a stepping stone for improvement.

You are part of a rock-solid support for your team that truly values their input. You create a sense of camaraderie and belonging that makes work feel like a second home. You have great relationships with your leaders, and your team members have great relationships with you. Your team experiences well-deserved recognition and opportunities for development all the time

Being loved means being open and honest in communications. Being part of the big decisions, knowing your work doesn't go unnoticed. It is those team adventures and the social events where team members turn into friends. You create and nurture those relationships and growth opportunities.

This culture you created is so supportive and attractive that top talent will flock to you and stick around. Loved leaders spark higher engagement and motivation and open doors to endless opportunities.

Let your team love you. Let them know you. Let them celebrate you. Embrace your team's love for you.

Benefits you will experience by being loved include *experiencing* the team's appreciation and loyalty for you. You will develop a better, stronger environment and experience personal fulfillment. You will attract talent and retain your team. Your team will be resilient and drive greater, more persistent innovation.

Some challenges you will experience include balancing emotional strain and conflict resolution. Being loved, you let your guard down and must be diligent about your boundaries. You inevitably have to navigate criticism while being fair in difficult decisions and maintaining consistency.

Some practical steps you can take to become loved include practicing listening and being transparent. You should show appreciation and inclusivity with your team while embracing humility. You need to be approachable and encourage growth. You need to open yourself up to be loved and be okay with being loved.

**Ideas to Demonstrate or Inspire:**
- *Random acts of kindness*: Encourage team members to perform random acts of kindness for one another.
- *Gratitude wall*: Create a wall where team members can post notes of gratitude and appreciation.
- *Mentorship programs*: Implement mentorship programs to support personal and professional growth.
- *Wellness initiatives*: Organize wellness activities such as yoga sessions, mindfulness workshops, or fitness challenges.

- *Personalized recognition*: Regularly recognize and celebrate individual and team achievements in personalized ways.
- *Team-building retreats*: Plan retreats focused on team building and relaxation.
- *Team member spotlights*: Feature team members in internal newsletters or meetings to highlight their contributions and stories.
- *Feedback Fridays*: Designate a day for open and constructive feedback sessions.

### Authentic People:
- Richard Branson: Loved for his adventurous spirit and business ventures.
- Audrey Hepburn: Loved for her elegance, acting talent, and humanitarian work.
- Robin Williams: Revered for his comedic genius and compassion.
- Chris Hemsworth: Loved for his acting and down-to-earth personality.

### Inspirational Voices:
- "How Art, Technology, and Design Inform Creative Leaders" by John Maeda: John explores the intersection of art, technology, and design, and how these fields can inspire creative leadership. He highlights the importance of curiosity and experimentation in driving innovation.
- "Build a Tower, Build a Team" by Tom Wujec: Tom discusses the "marshmallow challenge," a team-building exercise that reveals insights into collaboration and creativity. He emphasizes the value of prototyping and learning from failures.
- "Every Kid Needs a Champion" by Rita Pierson: Rita, a lifelong educator, shares the importance of building strong relationships and believing in the potential of every individual. Her talk underscores the transformative power of love and encouragement in leadership.

## Be Loving

For me, being loving means I embrace people within everything they choose to be, as they are, in full compassion and humanity. I engage with my team in deep care. I let them know and I tell them I love them. I draw my team into me and one another. My team develops a tight integration with one another and extends the love, appreciation, and respect for one another.

Loving

When you are loving, you are passionate about life. You love people. You thrive on helping and serving others. You have a heart full of empathy and kindness. You deeply care for everyone around you. You prioritize the emotional and mental well-being of your team. You create an atmosphere bursting with trust and mutual respect.

You are that beacon of compassion and understanding. You make the workplace a place where everyone feels included and loved. You embrace every opportunity to show care and concern for everyone around you. You treat everyone with kindness and compassion. Respect is at the core of the community you are building, where everyone thrives.

Empathy is your secret weapon. You dive into someone else's world and understanding their perspective. Being open-minded, you listen without judgment. You create a safe space. You experience people stories and make magic happen.

You acknowledge the hard work and contributions of your team with a simple, "Thank you," or a shout-out for their efforts. You are there to lend a helping hand/or word of encouragement.

You are mindful of what you say and do. You avoid gossip and negative talk. You build positive, uplifting relationships. You respect cultural and personal differences. Your mindful actions set a harmonious tone and create a loving workplace.

You transform lives. You are supportive and compassionate. You boost team morale and satisfaction. Your approach forges stronger relationships. Open communication, trust, and collaboration are ever present. This leads to higher productivity and endless innovation. As a bonus—people stick around in places where they feel truly valued.

Benefits you will experience by being loving include enhanced team morale and relationship enrichment. Communication will improve along with productivity and team-member retention rates. You and your team will develop a sense of belonging, of work family.

Some challenges you will experience include balancing compassion, love, and discipline. It is possible that team members may misinterpret intentions and be resistance to being embraced and/or change. The emotional labor can be intense, and loving people draws on many parts of you. Most importantly, it is absolutely critical that you maintain professional boundaries—*do not get lost here*. If you cannot manage loving your team carefully, then make sure to have open discussions with your team and aggressively manage boundaries. The consequences of getting this wrong are not insignificant—and it can go wrong in a hurry!

Some practical steps you can take to become loving include practicing active listening and encouraging open, accepting communication. You should actively and exceedingly demonstrate appreciation and empathy. Offer constructive feedback and underpin all communications with integrity and transparency. Demonstrate and acknowledge gratitude and provide resources for well-being.

### Ideas to Demonstrate or Inspire:
- *Gratitude wall*: Create a space where team members can post notes of appreciation for each other.
- *Random acts of kindness day*: Encourage team members to perform and recognize acts of kindness.
- *Wellness programs*: Offer programs that support physical, mental, and emotional health.
- *Team bonding activities*: Organize activities that build trust and camaraderie.
- *Team member recognition programs*: Regularly acknowledge and reward team members for their contributions.

- *Open-door policy*: Ensure leaders are approachable and available to discuss any concerns.
- *Support groups*: Establish groups where team members can share and support each other on various topics.
- *Charity involvement*: Encourage and facilitate team participation in charitable events.

**Authentic People:**
- Mother Teresa: Dedicated her life to caring for the poor and sick.
- Michael Jordan: Inspires and mentors young athletes.
- Matt Damon: Co-founder of Water.org, focusing on clean water access.

**Inspirational Voices:**
- "Why We Do What We Do" by Tony Robbins: Tony explores the forces that drive human behavior and how leaders can harness these forces to inspire and motivate their teams.
- "Start with Why—How Great Leaders Inspire Action" by Simon Sinek: Simon discusses the importance of purpose-driven leadership and how starting with "why" can inspire action.
- "The Optimism Bias" by Tali Sharot: Tali explores the optimism bias and its implications for leadership, emphasizing the need for hope and positivity.
- "Your Elusive Creative Genius" by Elizabeth Gilbert: Elizabeth discusses the creative process and the role of love and encouragement in nurturing creativity.

## Be Open-Minded

For me, being open-minded means knowing what I know, believing what I believe, and being open to changing my mind or absorbing differing methods, views, or approaches that I have not known or have resisted, following robust, fulfilling discussions. I remain dogmatically

Open-Minded

open to learning why my ways and knowledge are either obsolete or not relevant. My team knows they are free to challenge me on any and all topics—it is rare for me to dig-in and say no.

When you are open-minded, you lead with a heart wide open and embrace new ideas. You are open to new perspectives and experiences. You welcome diverse viewpoints and adapt to changes. You create an inclusive environment around these viewpoints. People feel heard.

You know you don't have all the answers and love it! You actively seek input from your team. You recognize that together the team is unstoppable. You're curious and flexible. You are always on the lookout for new ways to learn and improve. You drive engagement forward, making sure everyone's voice is heard.

You consider and value diverse perspectives. You listen actively and respect opinions. You are always learning. Magic happens when different ideas come together; you get innovative solutions and better decision-making. This thought diversity helps you identify blind spots and biases. You lead into well-rounded, effective strategies.

You create a culture of respect and understanding. People feel safe to share their unique perspectives with you. Your teams typically tackle any challenge.

You are open-minded professionally and personally too. By embracing different viewpoints, you continually expand your knowledge. You challenge your beliefs and seek a deeper understanding of the world. You are an incredibly adaptable, well-rounded team member.

You allow for the free exchange of ideas. You foster growth across your team and company. You fuel innovation and encouraging exploration of new ideas. You build cohesive teams exuding respect and values. You are equipped to navigate complex and uncertain environments. You adapt to new information and changing circumstances.

Benefits you will experience by being open-minded include enhanced motivation and better decision-making, increased adaptability, and stronger team cohesion. You will also experience improved team-member engagement.

Some challenges you will experience include information overload and decision paralysis through the ongoing introduction of new ideas. You will experience resistance to change and battle to maintain authority. Time management will be difficult through the ongoing discussion and discovery of ideas; knowing when to stop is critical.

Some practical steps you can take to become open-minded include seeking ongoing open-minded, diverse, creative, and novel feedback and guidance. Reflect on idea bias, challenge conventional and/or traditional thinking or methodologies. Conduct brain-storming sessions and host open forum discussions. Incentivize the adoption of novel ideas and continuous learning.

### Ideas to Demonstrate or Inspire:
- *Organize cross-departmental brainstorming sessions*: Facilitate sessions where team members from different departments collaborate on projects.
- *Create an anonymous suggestion box*: Allow team members to submit ideas and feedback anonymously.
- *Implement flexible work policies*: Offer remote work options, flexible hours, and job-sharing arrangements.
- *Celebrate cultural diversity with themed events*: Organize events that celebrate different cultures and traditions.
- *Encourage job rotation and shadowing opportunities*: Allow team members to experience different roles within the organization.

### Authentic People:
- Justin Trudeau: Advocated for diversity and inclusion in Canadian politics and society.
- Ruth Bader Ginsburg: Advocated for gender equality and open-minded jurisprudence.
- Billie Jean King: Fought for gender equality in sports and beyond.
- Megan Rapinoe: Advocated for LGBTQ+ rights and gender equality in sports.
- Jack Ma: Promoted entrepreneurship and innovation with Alibaba Group.

88 | LEADING MAGNANIMOUSLY

Inspirational Voices:
- "How to Make Stress Your Friend" by Kelly McGonigal: Kelly discusses how reframing stress can lead to better health and performance, highlighting the importance of an open-minded perspective.
- "How to Live Before You Die" by Steve Jobs: Steve shares personal stories about following one's intuition and being open to life's opportunities and challenges.
- "The Surprising Science of Happiness" by Dan Gilbert: Dan discusses how happiness can be synthesized and the importance of an open-minded approach to achieving it.
- "The Future We're Building—and Boring" by Elon Musk: Elon discusses his visionary projects and the importance of being open to ambitious, transformative ideas.
- "How to Build a Company Where the Best Ideas Win" by Ray Dalio: Ray shares principles for creating an idea meritocracy, highlighting the importance of being open to diverse viewpoints in business.

## Be Passionate

For me, being passionate is losing myself in the love of people and ideas. I believe passion draws people out magnetically. I am an all-out or all-in person. If I am in, there is nearly nothing that can stop me, and the earth will need to come to a near end before I abandon. I dedicate myself to the people around me to the cost of myself with the knowledge

Passionate

that their brilliance is my reward and that paying it forward is a thing. This absolute unyielding dedication to my team and their growth has yielded phenomenal human beings that, beyond me, excel in their own worlds and grow beyond their wildest dreams. Passion is contagious.

When you are passionate, your days brim with excitement for what lies ahead. You exude intense, electrifying dedication to work and mission. You dive headfirst into your vision and let your boundless energy and enthusiasm sweep others along with you. You are driven by passion. No obstacle is too big or small, no challenge too tough. You are the spark that lights up your team. You push them to new heights. The joy and emotional investment from you pour into everything you do.

Being passionate is a lifestyle for you. It is a way of being. You are completely engaged and invested in things that bring you purpose and fulfillment. Whether it is a hobby, cause, or sports, passion drives you to spend countless hours perfecting your craft simply because you love it. You share the love for that with others through warmth of connection and purpose.

Passion ignites in causes you deeply care about. You pour your time and energy into making a positive impact. This creates ripples of change in your communities. You have a fire inside of you and use it to make a difference. You have a heart full of determination and perseverance. You don't back down when things get tough. You use those challenges as fuel to drive you forward.

You bring that vibrant enthusiasm into everything you do. You feel deeply connected to your job and the company goals. You become the dynamo that drives success. Your energy is infectious, lifting everyone around you.

You are fully engaged and driven by a sense of purpose. You see the bigger picture and know your role's impact on the team's success. You create a positive and productive atmosphere. Your passion fosters a culture of innovation and growth.

You are always on the lookout for new challenges and opportunities to expand your skills. You are not afraid to take risks and step out of your comfort zone. Let your passion blaze brightly. Embrace it. Live it. Ignite the moment.

Benefits you will experience by being passionate include incredibly high engagement with your team and, as a result, between your team. Your passion will create passion.

Some challenges you will experience include the risk of burnout and overcommitment. Being passionate can be intensely draining; the emotional intensity can be extreme. Balancing passion with objectivity is difficult.

Some practical steps you can take to become passionate include finding your purpose and reason for passion. Cultivate your team's passion along with your own. Communicate effectively and caringly. Foster a supportive environment with your team and peers. Engage inspirationally and with energy. Recognize and celebrate achievements and show a deep and genuine interest in your team, their activities, and the company.

Ideas to Demonstrate or Inspire:
- *Passion projects*: Encourage team members to dedicate time to projects they are passionate about.
- *Storytelling sessions*: Share personal stories of passion and perseverance.
- *Mentorship programs*: Pair passionate leaders with team members to inspire and guide them.
- *Recognition programs*: Acknowledge and celebrate passionate efforts and achievements.
- *Innovation labs*: Create spaces where team members can brainstorm and work on innovative ideas.
- *Team challenges*: Organize challenges that align with the company's mission and values.

Authentic People:
- Abraham Lincoln: Passionate about preserving the Union and ending slavery.
- Peyton Manning: Passionate about football strategy and leadership.
- Leonardo DiCaprio: Passionate about acting and environmental activism.
- Lady Gaga: Passionate about music and mental health advocacy.
- Hugh Jackman: Known for his passionate commitment to acting and philanthropy.

Inspirational Voices:
- "How Great Leaders Inspire Action" by Simon Sinek: Simon explores the concept of the "Golden Circle" and how leaders can inspire action by focusing on the "why" behind their actions. He emphasizes

that passionate leaders communicate their vision effectively, creating a sense of purpose and motivation among their followers.
- "Grit: The Power of Passion and Perseverance" by Angela Lee Duckworth: Angela explains how grit, a combination of passion and perseverance, is a key predictor of success. She emphasizes that passionate leaders demonstrate resilience and long-term commitment to their goals.
- "Why We Do What We Do" by Tony Robbins: Tony delves into the psychology behind motivation and behavior. He discusses how passionate leaders understand and leverage their emotions to drive themselves and others toward success.

## Be Patient

For me, being patient is like pulling a hen's teeth when it comes to nearly everything in life, until I am engaged with individuals who want to find a better tomorrow and demonstrate ownership of self. With this, I have an eternity to help people, from my team to mentees in Africa, the USA, and India. I have all the time, patience, and energy in the world for people who want to grow. My life experience to date places me in a great position to give rounded insights and assistance. On the counterbalance—I don't suffer fools lightly.

Patient

When you are patient, you stay cool and composed. You are utterly in control regardless of the challenge. You embrace self-control and listen deeply. You do not make rushed decisions. You understand that real progress takes time and that setbacks are simply stepping stones on the path to greatness. You prioritize long-term success over tempting short-term wins. You build a culture that thrives on growth and resilience.

Growing people is like tending a garden for you. You have got the wisdom and experience. Your team is still learning, still getting their hands dirty. Your team needs time to burn their fingers. They need to figure out what you already know. And you, wait! Your patient heart is there for the long haul. You know this is about investing in people. You recognize that everyone grows at their own pace. You know that pace can change over time.

You are the calm in the storm—the rock when things get shaky. You control your emotions. You approach every task and interaction with an open mind. You approach situations and people with a serene spirit. You know everything will unfold in its own time. Forcing growth is sure to break something.

You understand that things won't always go according to plan. Your team member and/or team might struggle and resist new concepts. You are resilient and adaptable. You are determined in guiding them through every twist and turn without losing your cool.

You are fully present and don't interrupt or rush. You show empathy and make sure your team feels understood and supported. You know everyone learns at their own pace. Your patience and understanding makes all the difference when progress is slower than expected.

You know each team member is unique and adapt your methods to fit the individual. You are flexible and encouraging. You boost confidence, especially when challenges arise. You ask insightful questions, giving them the time and space to reflect.

You allow your team to stumble, using those moments as opportunities for growth. You adjust your strategies and remain steadfastly flexible with your expectations. You celebrate small wins and keep the focus on progress. You are a solid source of support for your team. You are all about sustainable growth and strong relationships. You nurture your team and give them the time to blossom.

Benefits you will experience by being patient include improved team morale and better decision-making. You will experience stronger relationships and increased productivity. Your team will experience enhanced problem-solving and a significant reduction in conflict and anxiety. You will see greater innovation and higher team-member retention

Some challenges you will experience include time-management challenges and a perception of weakness. You need to balance patience with action and understanding. You will face difficult situations and need to manage your composure along with team and leadership expectations.

Some practical steps you can take to become patient include practicing active listening and developing your emotional intelligence. You need to set realistic goals and embrace mindfulness. Your team requires active feedback and the ability to reflect on experiences without the introduction of stressors. Stress management is a key activity for you and the team. Reflect on experiences, learnings, and mistakes while setting realistic, achievable goals and deadlines.

### Ideas to Demonstrate or Inspire:
- *Mentorship programs*: Establishing mentorship programs where experienced team members guide newer ones.
- *Mindfulness workshops*: Organizing workshops to teach mindfulness and stress management techniques.
- *Flexible deadlines*: Implementing flexible deadlines for projects to reduce stress and encourage thoughtful work.
- *Recognition systems*: Creating systems to recognize and reward patient and thoughtful problem-solving.
- *Team-building activities*: Conducting activities that promote collaboration and patience among team members.
- *Open feedback sessions*: Having regular feedback sessions to discuss progress and challenges in a calm and constructive manner.
- *Learning opportunities*: Offering opportunities for continuous learning and professional development.
- *Inclusive decision-making*: Involving team members in decision-making processes to ensure all voices are heard.

### Authentic People:
- Golda Meir: Demonstrated patience in her role as prime minister of Israel during difficult times.
- Lech Wałęsa: Patience in his efforts to lead Poland out of communism.
- Dalai Lama: Exemplifies patience through his lifelong dedication to peace and compassion.

- Sachin Tendulkar: Exemplified patience throughout his cricket career.
- Chris Pratt: Demonstrated patience in his career progression from television to blockbuster films.

Inspirational Voices:
- "The Happy Secret to Better Work" by Shawn Achor: Highlights how patience and positivity can enhance leadership and productivity. Shawn discusses the relationship between happiness and success, suggesting that a positive and patient mindset leads to greater productivity and effective leadership.
- "The Beauty of Being a Misfit" by Lidia Yuknavitch: Discusses the power of patience and resilience in embracing one's uniqueness. Lidia shares her personal journey of feeling like a misfit and how patience and resilience helped her embrace her uniqueness and achieve success.
- "Why Some of Us Don't Have One True Calling" by Emilie Wapnick: Highlights the role of patience in exploring multiple passions and career paths. Emilie discusses the concept of multipotentiality and how patience in exploring diverse interests can lead to a fulfilling and dynamic career.

## Be Persistent

For me, being persistent is like being the dog that caught the tire of a car slowly driving down the street—I don't stop. If we agree on an approach, deliverable, or goal—I don't let up. I am persistent about driving deliverables and outcomes, in helping people achieve more than they dream, and in chasing the deal or learning a new skill. This quality of just not stopping and tiring people out has bitten me a few times, too.

Persistent

When you are persistent, you are consistently going after your goals, no matter what challenges or setbacks life throws at you. You keep that fire burning with resilience no matter the odds. Persistent is your superpower

You are determined and unwavering. Your eyes are always on the prize. Your commitment to your vision and goals is not just about you. Your energy and enthusiasm are contagious. You continuously motivate everyone around.

You have that never-give-up attitude. No matter how many times you get knocked down, you get right back up. You are resilient and adaptable. You always find a way to turn obstacles into opportunities. You work smart, constantly seeking solutions.

You create a team culture where everyone is inspired by your relentless drive. You celebrate small wins and keep everyone focused. You are open-minded and fun-loving. You are ready to adjust your sails at a minute's notice, but never your destination.

You know when to switch gears and find new paths. You understand that sometimes the message just needs a different approach. You are in tune with your team and aware of their needs. You are always working to find the right way to connect and inspire.

Being dynamically persistent is your secret weapon. You are resilient and adaptable. You thrive in a constantly changing environment. You lead with passion. You love helping and serving people.

You inspire your team to build their own resilience and tenacity. You set a powerful, unwavering example that any challenge can be an opportunity for growth. You create a culture where everyone sees obstacles as stepping stones. You know that together, the team is unstoppable. Keep pushing forward. Keep inspiring.

Benefits you will experience by being persistent include increased resilience to challenges along with enhanced problem-solving. You will naturally experience a higher level of achievement and be an inspiration for team cohesion. Your persistence will be an inspiration and motivation for others to drive forward.

Some challenges you will experience include the risk of burnout and perceived stubbornness. You will face resource constraints and team-member and leader frustrations due to your tenacity and drive. Not many will keep up with you, and you will need to maintain morale while being flexible and knowing when to let go and/or stop.

Some practical steps you can take to become persistent include setting clear long-term goals and developing resilience. Stay positive and encourage feedback, celebrating small wins. Stay focused and build a supporting network. Remember to manage stress and creative problem-solving, and do not be afraid to adjust strategies when needed.

Ideas to Demonstrate or Inspire:
- *Persistence awards*: Create a recognition program for team members who demonstrate persistence.
- *Storytelling sessions*: Share stories of persistence from team members or famous personalities.
- *Mentorship programs*: Establish mentorship programs where persistent leaders guide others.
- *Resilience workshops*: Organize workshops focused on building resilience and persistence.
- *Persistence challenges*: Set up challenges that require persistence to complete.
- *Regular feedback*: Implement a system for regular feedback to encourage continuous improvement.
- *Team-building activities*: Plan activities that require teamwork and persistence.
- *Resource support*: Provide resources and support for long-term projects.

Authentic People:
- Angela Merkel: Led Germany through multiple crises with unwavering determination.
- Ronald Reagan: Overcame numerous obstacles to implement significant policy changes as US president.
- Steve Jobs: Persisted in revolutionizing technology with Apple despite early failures.
- Robert Downey Jr.: Persisted in overcoming personal struggles to revive his acting career.

**Inspirational Voices:**
- "The Power of Believing That You Can Improve" by Carol Dweck: Carol explains the concept of the growth mindset, which is the belief that abilities can be developed through dedication and hard work. She shares how adopting a growth mindset can foster persistence and resilience, leading to greater success and personal fulfillment.
- "How the Worst Moments in Our Lives Make Us Who We Are" by Andrew Solomon: Andrew discusses how personal struggles and adversity shape our identities. He highlights the role of persistence in overcoming challenges and finding meaning and strength in difficult experiences.
- "The Surprising Habits of Original Thinkers" by Adam Grant: Adam explores the habits of original thinkers, including the role of persistence in bringing innovative ideas to life. He shares insights on how to nurture creativity and resilience in oneself and others.

### Be Predictable

For me, being predictable is being known. My team knows what I am going to do in what situations, with what knowledge and urgency. They know when I have answers or not, and they know when I will replay their questions and concerns to them and wait for them to engage and/or decide. My team trusts that no matter what they bring to me, I will engage in the same way—every time.

Predictable

When you are predictable, you create a work environment where your team knows exactly what to expect from you. Your confidence and trust blossoms when your actions and reactions are consistent and reliable. You are a rock for your team. Your consistent behavior and clear communication set the stage for a stable and trustworthy atmosphere. Your team can anticipate your moves. This reduces uncertainty and boosts their confidence in your leadership.

You consistently show up with the same positive energy. You meet deadlines and follow through on promises. You maintain an upbeat attitude. You are always present in the same way, every time, whether it is fun or work, whether risk mitigation or a cup of coffee, regardless of the time of day or location. Your team values this. They know they can rely on you. That sense of stability makes being in the workplace a joy.

You create a safe base from which your team can explore new ideas and take bold steps. Your team knows what to expect from you. This trust and dependability makes communication a breeze. Interactions are more transparent and meaningful.

Your role has a profound impact on your team's growth and well-being. Your team looks up to you for guidance and inspiration. Your team knows you have got their backs.

Your team is more likely to be open to transparency when they know how you'll respond in various situations. You bring stability and trust to your team. They know what to expect. They feel secure and empowered. Your consistency sets clear expectations and goals. Embrace predictability as a foundation for excitement and innovation.

Benefits you will experience by being predictable include the development and building of trust and a reduction in anxiety. You will experience improved communication, stability, and enhanced decision-making. Your team will start echoing similar traits and become predictable as a cohesive group.

Some challenges you will experience include perceived rigidity and resistance to change. You may well experience boredom in some spaces and become overdependent on the problems you are chasing, the method of delivery, and/or the people around you. You may well experience the misinterpretation of your intentions and approach by people expecting alternate agendas. You may also face a perception of perfectionism or having all the answers.

Some practical steps you can take to become predictable include establishing clear goals and consistently communicating. Model your desired behavior and provide regular feedback and transparency on decision-making. Adhere to established processes and change them as the processes become obsolete along with your execution methodology. Follow through on your promises

### Ideas to Demonstrate or Inspire:
- *Implement routine check-ins*: Regularly scheduled one-on-one meetings.
- *Establish clear protocols*: Develop and follow standard operating procedures.
- *Create a consistent recognition program*: Regularly recognize and reward achievements.
- *Set and maintain office hours*: Be consistently available during specific times.
- *Develop a transparent communication plan*: Give regular updates on company goals and progress.

### Authentic People:
- Angela Merkel: Known for her steady and predictable approach to governance.
- Tom Brady: Known for his consistent winning performance.
- Usain Bolt: Predictable speed and success in sprinting.
- Jackie Joyner Kersee: Predictable excellence in track and field.
- Denzel Washington: Consistent high-quality performances.
- Sandra Bullock: Predictable excellence in film.

### Inspirational Voices:
- "Lead Like the Great Conductors" by Itay Talgam: Itay uses the metaphor of conducting to illustrate the power of consistent leadership in guiding a team.
- "Tribal Leadership" by David Logan: David explains how leaders can build and lead tribes, emphasizing the importance of consistent values and behavior.
- "The Difference Between Winning and Succeeding" by John Wooden: John discusses his philosophy of success, highlighting the role of consistent effort and integrity.

- "How to Run a Company with (Almost) No Rules" by Ricardo Semler: Ricardo shares his approach to leadership, which includes consistent trust and empowerment of team members.
- "Extreme Ownership" by Jocko Willink: Jocko emphasizes the importance of taking responsibility consistently in leadership.

### Be Present

For me, being present is being here, with you, right now, always. I ensure that when I am engaged with my team, I am with them wholly and comprehensively. This means I hear and absorb the discussions and energies, the desires and intents of the people I engage with. While I suck at attention to detail and am bloody fast at getting stuff done, I am present in the work I do. My awareness has placed me in a position where I am naturally intuitive in what I should be fully present on and what I should delegate or run from.

Present

When you are present, you bring your vibrant self to every interaction with your team. You are totally engaged, right here. You give your undivided attention to your team members and the tasks at hand. You listen actively and interact genuinely. You are the heartbeat of your team's dynamic. You are approachable and empathetic. You create collaborative environments where everyone thrives and are fully aware.

You dive into every task and interaction with your whole self. You vest yourself physically and emotionally, show up in meetings, and are present in discussions. You engage in projects with full enthusiasm and focus. You are in the moment and tuned into the needs and perspectives of those around you.

You actively participate in meetings and discussions. You knock out tasks on time and are on meeting deadlines like a boss. You are open to new ideas and perspectives and adapt to changing circumstances quickly. You are empathetic and supportive toward your colleagues and create an atmosphere where everyone feels heard and valued.

You set aside distractions and immerse yourself in the here and now. You listen without judgment and have fun together. You are there for the team emotionally and physically. You build strong bonds and deep relationships, understand your team's needs, and engage in their interests. You understand and are mindful of their emotions.

You create a sense of security and stability. Your team feels safe and valued, which allows them to thrive. Your presence fosters trust and respect. You understand your team's challenges and needs. You are able to drive effective problem-solving and decision-making and be fully engaged and in tune with your team.

Benefits you will experience by being present include enhanced trust and improved communication. You will develop stronger relationships and drive higher morale. Your team will experience better decision-making and increased productivity. You will observe reduced stress and greater innovation.

Some challenges you will experience include time management challenges and emotional drain. You need to learn to set boundaries and maintain focus, consistently.

Some practical steps you can take to become present include practicing active listening and obtaining mindfulness training. Regularly check in with yourself and your mentor to see if you are overworking and overcommitting; give yourself a break. Practice empathy and transparency and work hard on delegation. Identify activities and projects you do and do not need to be involved in, and celebrate milestones.

### Ideas to Demonstrate or Inspire:
- *Mindfulness workshops*: Offer mindfulness and meditation sessions.
- *Open office hours*: Set specific times for team members to discuss anything.
- *Team-building retreats*: Organize retreats focusing on presence and engagement.
- *Feedback circles*: Regular feedback sessions to share thoughts and ideas.

- *Inclusive decision-making*: Involve team members in important decisions.
- *Celebrating achievements*: Publicly acknowledge team successes.
- *Empathy training*: Provide training on empathy and active listening.
- *Personal development plans*: Create development plans for each team member.

### Authentic People:
- Winston Churchill: His wartime leadership showed resilience and presence.
- Cory Booker: Known for his active engagement and presence in the community.
- Lewis Hamilton: Recognized for his present leadership in Formula 1 racing.
- Meg Whitman: Known for her presence and leadership at HP and eBay.

### Inspirational Voices:
- "Say Your Truths and Seek Them in Others" by Elizabeth Lesser: Elizabeth explores the concept of "open-heartedness," which involves being present and truthful in our interactions. She encourages leaders to be honest and open, fostering deeper connections and understanding.
- "Looking Past Limits" by Caroline Casey: Caroline shares her journey of overcoming blindness and redefining her identity. She emphasizes the importance of being present and fully embracing who we are, regardless of limitations. Casey's story inspires leaders to be authentic and fully engaged in their lives.
- "10 Ways to Have a Better Conversation" by Celeste Headlee: Celeste offers practical advice on how to have meaningful conversations by being fully present. She discusses the importance of listening, asking good questions, and being genuinely interested in others. Headlee's talk emphasizes the value of presence in building strong connections.

## Be Purposeful

For me, being purposeful is what is expected of me and, beyond intent, knowing what I am doing has a purpose and how it ties to the larger mission of my team. I become a wicked prickly pear if my or my team's activities are not purposeful. I want to puke on meandering tasks, responsibilities, and activities. Watching team members (direct or not) putter around in the dark through self-decision or leadership direction nearly drives me to insanity—especially when the participant is aware of it and chooses willful blindness or absolution of behavior.

Purposeful

When you are purposeful, you absolutely buzz with purpose—a clear and electrifying sense of direction. You have a deep, heartfelt commitment to smashing meaningful goals. You align all actions and decisions with your core values and bold vision. You connect the dots between your mission and each team member's role. You create an incredible sense of collective purpose felt to the bone.

You understand your goals and charge toward them with passion and intention. You make decisions that matter and understand how your work fits into the bigger picture. You recognize the ripple effect of your actions on everyone around you. You are open to different perspectives and actively seek out diverse viewpoints. You goal is to make decisions that are inclusive and well-rounded.

You set realistic yet exciting goals! You break them down into bite-sized, actionable steps. You continually evaluate and tweak them as you go. You own your actions and take responsibility. You are always mindful of the impact you are making. You have a clear direction and are aware of how you affect others. You relentlessly work toward goals that sync up with your company's mission and values.

You inspire your team with a sense of meaning and direction. Your motivation is a game-changer for engagement and productivity. With clear purpose, you and your team tackle obstacles head-on. You remain laser focused. You align your team's goals and values with those of the company and fostering a tight-knit, collaborative environment. You look to make a positive impact and leave a lasting legacy. You goal is to drive both your personal and professional worlds forward.

You have a clear understanding of your goals and actively work toward achieving them. This involves being intentional and focused on your actions and decisions, aligning them with the overall mission and objectives of the organization.

You inspire your team by providing a sense of meaning and direction. Your team is better equipped to navigate obstacles and stay focused during tough times. You strive to make a positive impact and leave a lasting legacy, contributing to both organizational success and societal well-being.

Benefits you will experience by being purposeful include enhanced engagement and improved performance. You will attract talent into a sustainable success model. Your deliverables will be all-enabling and correlated to a mission and vision tying into company priorities.

Some challenges you will experience include balancing short-term and long-term goals and overcoming associated resistance. Communicating with purpose is key, as is staying true to values.

Some practical steps you can take to become purposeful include defining your purpose and communicating it clearly. Be sure to align your actions with purpose and encourage active participation. Empower your team members and engage in regular reflection and reviews. Encourage continuous collaboration and learning.

### Ideas to Demonstrate or Inspire:
- *Purpose workshops*: Host workshops to help team members connect personal goals with organizational purpose.
- *Storytelling sessions*: Share stories of how the organization's work impacts the community.
- *Purpose-driven projects*: Initiate projects that align with the organization's mission and values.
- *Recognition programs*: Recognize and reward team members who demonstrate alignment with the organization's purpose

- *Purpose retreats*: Organize retreats focused on reflecting and strategizing around the organization's purpose.
- *Guest speakers*: Invite speakers who embody purposeful leadership to inspire the team.
- *Community involvement*: Encourage and facilitate team member participation in community service.

### Authentic People:
- Jawaharlal Nehru: Worked toward modernizing India.
- Lech Walesa: Led Poland's Solidarity movement for democracy.
- Bill Gates: Revolutionized personal computing and philanthropy.
- Rihanna: Supported global education and emergency response efforts.
- Bono: Advocated for poverty reduction and AIDS awareness.
- Mark Ruffalo: Advocated for environmental protection and renewable energy.

### Inspirational Voices:
- "Start with Why" by Simon Sinek: Simon explains the concept of the "Golden Circle" and emphasizes the importance of understanding and communicating the purpose behind actions. Sinek provides examples of successful organizations and leaders who lead with purpose, encouraging others to focus on their core motivations.
- "Why We Do What We Do" by Tony Robbins: Tony delves into the psychological factors that drive human behavior. He emphasizes the importance of understanding our motivations and purpose in life to achieve fulfillment.
- "The Power of Believing That You Can Improve" by Carol Dweck: Carol introduces the concept of a growth mindset, emphasizing the importance of believing in one's ability to improve and grow. She argues that leaders who cultivate a growth mindset are more likely to inspire and motivate their teams.

- "Which Country Does the Most Good for the World?" by Simon Anholt: Simon presents the Good Country Index, which ranks countries based on their contributions to global well-being. He argues that leaders should be purposeful in their policies, focusing on the greater good rather than just national interests.

## Be a Servant

I am a servant. I put my team's and company's priorities and importance ahead of mine—period. I knowingly do this at my own peril and cost, and I sleep well with myself. I acknowledge that I am part of a minority of people who will sacrifice self to the extent I do for the benefit of others, from salary to personal brand to skills to training public speaking, all the way through to my most favored or desired job. I am perfectly okay with this and yield my gratification and life success from the success of the people I service. Yes, I know—I take this too far, but I really do sleep well despite the personal impacts. I encourage you to serve, be a servant, to whatever level is most relevant to you. As a leader, your number one priority is to serve those who report to you—in every manner they need it—*not* to the limits of what you decide it to be.

Servant

When you are a servant, you make everyone feel valued, heard, and supported. You are a guide and mentor. You are here for other people; your mission is to help others no matter what. There are few directions your support for your team and peers will not go. You look after and help others on a range of topics. You flip the script on traditional leadership by putting the needs and growth of your team at the forefront. You are all about empathy and listening. You are a steward of your team with a deep sense of personal commitment.

Your main goal is to uplift and empower your team. It is not about you; it is about them. You are there to serve and support, focusing on the well-being and development of each team member. This means putting their needs first and using your position to help them shine.

Your job is to create a positive and inclusive work environment where everyone feels valued and supported. You actively listen to your team's concerns and provide the resources they need. You show empathy and compassion and lead through acts of service and kindness. You nurture trust and enhance morale. You build a culture of mutual respect and support.

Integrity and humility are your best friends. You roll up your sleeves and work alongside your team. You show them you are not afraid to get your hands dirty and that you value their contributions. This approach promotes trust and collaboration and creates a sense of community. Your team will be more engaged and productive because they know you are in it with them.

You empower your team, providing opportunities for growth and learning. You delegate responsibilities and trust their members' decisions. You recognize and value their diverse perspectives and strengths. You encourage open communication and collaboration. Your role is to mentor and support them.

You celebrate and embrace different views and methods. You create a safe space where people feel comfortable sharing ideas. You actively seek out and listen to differing viewpoints. You put others first and create a supportive, inclusive environment. You inspire and empower your team to reach their full potential.

You focus on long-term goals and the well-being of your team and company. This balanced approach helps you navigate challenges and achieve lasting impact. By encouraging open dialogue and collaboration, you foster a dynamic and creative environment.

Teams led by you often show higher performance and increased motivation. You promote trust and respect. You demonstrate ethical behavior and attract top talent. You encourage diverse perspectives, and open communication fosters innovation and problem-solving.

You prioritize the needs, growth, and well-being of others above your own ambitions. Your leadership style, characterized by empathy, listening, and stewardship, creates an inclusive environment.

Benefits you will experience by being a servant include maximizing team dedication and performance. You will increase team-member satisfaction, and retention, and drive an incredibly strong team culture. You will invigorate innovation and create a self-sustaining, success-driven culture.

Some challenges you will experience include potential burnout and the need for time management. You need to balance the perception of weakness and manage slow decision-making. You need to manage your energy and passion and be all-aware of your personal and professional impacts as you find the healthy balance of your version of serving.

Some practical steps you can take to become a servant include encouraging growth and building a community. You must act with humility and be empathetic—always. Find a mentor or life coach who can help you be self-aware and grow—the counterbalance is incredibly important for a servant. Promote ethical behavior and empower decision-making. Empower others, teach others, and serve with a willful, loving heart.

Ideas to Demonstrate or Inspire:
- *Volunteer days*: Organize team volunteer events for community service.
- *Mentorship programs*: Establish formal mentoring for professional growth.
- *Recognition systems*: Create ways to acknowledge and reward team contributions.
- *Open forums*: Host regular meetings where team members can voice concerns and ideas.
- *Personal development plans*: Support individual career goals and training.
- *Flexible working arrangements*: Allow remote work or flexible hours.
- *Health and wellness initiatives*: Promote physical and mental well-being.
- *Inclusive decision-making*: Involve team members in strategic planning.
- *Skill-sharing sessions*: Encourage team members to share their expertise.

**Authentic People:**
- Mahatma Gandhi: Gandhi led India to independence through non-violent resistance, emphasizing humility, empathy, and serving the masses.
- Mother Teresa: Though not a traditional politician, Mother Teresa's humanitarian work and service to the poor and sick exemplify servant leadership.
- Dalai Lama: The Dalai Lama advocates for peace, compassion, and human rights.
- Herb Kelleher: Kelleher prioritized team member satisfaction and customer service.
- Bono: The U2 frontman has focused on global poverty and health initiatives.

**Inspirational Voices:**
- "Why Good Leaders Make You Feel Safe" by Simon Sinek: Simon explains how servant leaders create environments where people feel safe and valued. Sinek provides examples of leaders who put their people first, illustrating how servant leadership can lead to greater organizational success.
- "Inspiring a Life of Immersion" by Jacqueline Novogratz: Jacqueline discusses her journey in social entrepreneurship and the importance of immersing oneself in the communities they serve. She highlights how servant leaders work alongside their teams and communities, listening and learning to make a meaningful impact.
- "Why Leaders Eat Last" by Simon Sinek: Simon discusses the concept of servant leadership, where leaders prioritize the needs of their team members. Sinek's talk highlights the importance of empathy and selflessness in leadership.

## Be Sincere

For me, being sincere means being a pane of glass—completely transparent and completely there. While I work persistently on this, it is not hard at all to be completely sincere with my team, paying a deep interest in their personal and professional lives. I love my team and could never show up in any other way. Like I said earlier—I like sleep well with myself and work hard to make it so—being sincere is foundational.

Sincere

When you are sincere, you are genuine and straightforward. You are real in every action and word. You are transparent and authentic and consistently show integrity. Your team feels your vibe and knows when you are being true to your values, making them feel valued and understood. This is a way of life for you: being true to yourself and to others without agendas. You build trust by embracing sincerity and integrity demonstrating you can be relied on, fostering open and honest communications.

You create a harmonious and just community around you and practice transparency and accountability for your actions. You promote a sense of responsibility and naturally foster a culture of empathy, allowing you to experience genuine interactions with your team on a deeper level.

You are genuine and honest in your actions and interactions, truthful in your words and deeds, and follow through on your commitments. You respect others' feelings and perspectives while staying open to different viewpoints, take responsibility for your actions, and admit to mistakes, fostering a positive and productive atmosphere where collaboration is natural.

Being sincere does not mean agreeing with others; it means being truthful and authentic even when it's tough. You allow for healthy and respectful debates and discussions and are trustworthy. Your clear intentions and authenticity help you maximize influence for the greater good.

You can't fake sincerity. You foster trust and credibility within your organization through strong, authentic relationships with all stakeholders. You lead with sincerity and are genuinely passionate and fun-loving.

Benefits you will experience by being sincere include the development and building of trust and increased engagement. You will experience better communication and enhanced credibility. Stronger, more trusting relationships will be self-evident.

Some challenges you will experience include a sense of vulnerability and the possibility of misunderstanding. You will need to balance transparency and emotional labor while being consistent in how you present yourself. Being sincere is not a part-time activity and is not something you can mask or pretend—it is either there or not.

Some practical steps you can take to become sincere include self-reflection and practicing active listening and empathy. You must communicate openly and honestly, admit mistakes, and practice empathy. Conduct regular team check-ins and implement open-door policies.

**Ideas to Demonstrate or Inspire:**
- *Honesty workshops*: Organize workshops focused on the importance of sincerity and honesty.
- *Open forums*: Hold regular open forums where team members can share their thoughts and feedback without fear.
- *Transparent communication channels*: Use platforms for open communication, like intranets or team collaboration tools.
- *Recognition programs*: Create programs that recognize and reward sincere behaviors.
- *Mentorship programs*: Encourage sincere leaders to mentor others, sharing their experiences and values.
- *Anonymous feedback*: Implement systems for anonymous feedback to encourage honest input from team members.
- *Personal development plans*: Develop personalized growth plans that focus on enhancing sincerity and authenticity.

Authentic People:
- Abraham Lincoln: Lincoln's sincere dedication to preserving the Union and ending slavery during the American Civil War highlighted his commitment to the principles of freedom and equality.
- Dalai Lama: The Dalai Lama's sincere advocacy for peace, compassion, and human rights has improved lives.
- Billie Jean King: King's sincere advocacy for gender equality in sports has had a lasting impact on tennis.
- Howard Schultz: Schultz's sincere commitment to social responsibility and team member welfare has shaped Starbucks' corporate culture.
- Tom Hanks: Hanks' sincere and down-to-earth demeanor has made him one of the most beloved actors.
- Jennifer Lawrence: Lawrence's sincere and candid public persona has endeared her to fans and made her a relatable figure in Hollywood.

Inspirational Voices:
- "What Makes a Good Life? Lessons from the Longest Study on Happiness" by Robert Waldinger: Robert Waldinger shares insights on the importance of sincere relationships and their impact on long-term happiness and leadership effectiveness.
- "Listening to Shame" by Brené Brown: Brené Brown discusses the connection between shame, vulnerability, and sincerity, explaining how leaders can embrace these aspects to build trust.
- "Dare to Disagree" by Margaret Heffernan: Margaret Heffernan discusses the role of sincerity in fostering constructive disagreement and innovation. She emphasizes the need for leaders to encourage honest dialogue.
- "The Surprising Science of Happiness" by Dan Gilbert: Dan Gilbert discusses how sincerity and authenticity contribute to genuine happiness and effective leadership.

## Be Transparent

For me, being transparent is like being a glass prism with the decoding manual on how and why different colors shine. I work to make sure there are leader message decoders – help interpret what leaders are giving guidance on with a purpose to make sure the teams do not end up with 5 different interpretations and assumed instructions.. My goal is to make sure that the one message that is intended or given is actually understood. For me, transparency is not about relaying what is said—it is about helping the person understand what is meant. Within this, I balance who is ready for what level of transparency.

Transparent

When you are transparent, you are an open book that shares information pervasively in near real time. You are as real as it gets and foster a vibe of trust and openness. You are upfront with your intentions and decisions, along with the rational context behind them. You make everyone feel valued and included and boost engagement and collaboration.

You are open and honest in everything you do, sharing knowledge and being accountable. You intensely listen to different perspectives and actively lead with transparency. You create a culture of trust and unity and ensure misunderstandings and conflicts become a thing of the past.

You are open about your company's goals and strategies, along with talking about the bumps in the road. You involve your team in decisions, making them feel like they belong, giving them a sense of ownership and empowerment.

You are real and present with your thoughts and feelings, sharing concerns and admitting when you need help. You are honest about your capabilities and limitations and promote a culture of safety for team members to share their thoughts and ideas. Your transparency creates a big, inclusive family where everyone's voice matters.

You are open about your thought processes and make yourself accessible and approachable, so your team feels comfortable coming to you with questions or concerns.

You are clear about your team's goals and expectations, communicating the team's objectives and how each person's role contributes to the big picture. You are open about challenges that pop up and discuss potential solutions as a team. This transparency aligns everyone's efforts and creates a sense of accountability and supportive collaboration.

You admit to and learn from mistakes as part of your transparency. By owning your errors, you demonstrate humility and vulnerability, encouraging team members to take ownership of their own mistakes, driving continuous improvement. Transparency facilitates better, smarter decision-making.

Benefits you will experience by being transparent include the development of trust and personal attention and participation. You will help every team member feel like an intimate part of the team. You will enhance collaboration and accountability and drive team-member engagement. Most of all, you will help the team members feel like they are part of the company—help them feel relevant.

Some challenges you will experience include the creation of vulnerability for you and the team. Transparency does not come for free, and, "Knowledge is power," can be liberating as well as daunting. You need to manage who gets what—and it can be incredibly overwhelming. Team members will misinterpret what you share and will require your hands to course correct. You will face inevitable complaints on the lack there-of, and then complaints of vagaries and lack of focus. You will need to find your own balance with your team.

Some practical steps you can take to become transparent include a strategy of communicating often and early. Be honest in your messaging and tell your team what you can and cannot talk about. Admit your and the company's mistakes as you share insights and information. Actively listen as you provide feedback. Be transparent on all topics the company has agreed on, including financials, recruitment, diversity, goals, mission, revenues, and opportunities.

Ideas to Demonstrate or Inspire:
- *Transparency days*: Dedicate a day each month for leaders to share updates and insights into company performance and decisions

- *Anonymous Q&A sessions*: Hold regular sessions where team members can ask questions anonymously, and leaders answer openly.
- *Open strategy meetings*: Allow team members to sit in on strategy meetings to understand decision-making processes.
- *Transparency training*: Provide training on the importance of transparency and how to practice it in daily work.
- *Suggestion box*: Implement a digital suggestion box where team members can submit ideas and feedback anonymously.
- *Open performance reviews*: Encourage leaders to share their performance review processes and results with their teams.
- *Town hall meetings*: Regularly hold town hall meetings where leaders share updates and take questions from team members.
- *Transparency portal*: Create an online portal where company performance data, goals, and progress are shared openly.
- *Leader blogs*: Encourage leaders to write regular blog posts about company updates, challenges, and successes.
- *Team member spotlights*: Highlight team members who demonstrate transparency in their work, fostering a culture of openness.

## Authentic People:

- Cristiano Ronaldo: Soccer player known for his transparent approach to his career and personal life.
- Naomi Osaka: Tennis player known for her transparent discussions on mental health.
- Elon Musk: CEO of Tesla known for his open communication on social media.
- Richard Branson: Founder of Virgin Group known for his openness and transparency.
- Jennifer Lawrence: Actress known for her openness and transparency about her experiences in Hollywood.

Inspirational Voices:
- "What It Takes to Be a Great Leader" by Roselinde Torres. Roselinde Torres discusses the key qualities of great leaders, emphasizing the importance of adaptability, transparency, and openness in leadership. She highlights how leaders can anticipate change and prepare for the future by being transparent with their teams.
- "The Happy Secret to Better Work" by Shawn Achor. Shawn Achor explores the connection between happiness and productivity, highlighting the role of transparent leadership in creating a positive and productive work environment.
- "The Tribes We Lead" by Seth Godin. Seth Godin discusses how leaders can inspire and lead by creating tribes based on shared values and transparent communication. He highlights the role of openness in building strong, cohesive teams.
- "How Great Leaders Inspire Action" by Simon Sinek. Simon Sinek introduces the concept of the "Golden Circle" and how leaders can inspire action by being transparent about their "why." He discusses the power of clear and open communication in leadership.

## **Be Understanding**

For me, being understanding validates my notion of accepting people as they are, as they want to be experienced, and allowing them to demonstrate and live themselves. This means I am open to and considerate of decisions team members make. It also means I work to understand why they do what they do in the way they do it. I try to understand them, their motivations, and their why. It is important for me to enter all situations with a mind to understand before I talk—be it with a team member, leader, customer, or partner.

Understanding

When you are understanding, you make every team member feel heard and valued, striving to ensure people are genuinely appreciated. You are an understanding leader and work to make it happen. You are a leader who truly gets people working hard by listening with your heart and soaking in every word as the most important thing in the world.

You create a space where everyone feels safe sharing their thoughts and dreams and talking about their concerns. Your team is a family that thrives on trust, openness, and a ton of fun.

You are about empathy and feeling what others feel, continually working to see the world through their eyes. You embrace the beautiful diversity of thoughts and backgrounds around you, being the go-to person for meaningful conversations. You love diving deep into different perspectives, so your engagement is beyond listening, making sure you are really hearing them.

You are curious and open-minded, embracing new ideas like they are the latest dance craze. You dive into different cultures and experiences with enthusiasm, showing everyone around you that every voice matters. You create a vibrant and inclusive space where creativity and collaboration soar.

Your team is motivated and united, with an inevitable increase in productivity. You prioritize empathy and active listening and resolve conflicts like a superstar, building solid relationships. You inspire loyalty that sticks and leads to happier team members and a lower turnover. You are a beacon of understanding. You show that you care and are there to listen.

Benefits you will experience by being understanding include improved team-member engagement and enhanced collaboration. You will experience higher retention rates and better conflict resolution. Trust will develop along with reciprocal understanding on your why."

Some challenges you will experience include being emotionally drained at the expense of time. You need to balance your energies and time and watch out for your own bias in approach, background, skills, etc. You may need to course correct decision-making as you come to understand more.

Some practical steps you can take to become understanding include practicing active listening and demonstrating empathy. Seek feedback while being patient and continue your transparent communication and engagement style. Cultivate emotional intelligence and remain open to learning—always.

### Ideas to Demonstrate or Inspire:
- *Empathy workshops*: Organize workshops that focus on developing empathy and active listening skills.
- *Open-door policy*: Encourage open communication by having an open-door policy for team members to voice their concerns and ideas.
- *Diversity and inclusion initiatives*: Create programs that celebrate and promote diversity and inclusion.
- *Team building activities*: Engage in activities that foster teamwork and understanding among team members.
- *Team member recognition programs*: Recognize and reward team members who demonstrate understanding and empathy.
- *Mentorship programs*: Establish mentorship programs that pair experienced team members with new hires to foster a supportive environment.
- *Conflict resolution training*: Provide training on effective conflict resolution techniques that emphasize understanding and empathy.

### Authentic People:
- Jacinda Ardern: Recognized for her empathetic response to crises.
- Eleanor Roosevelt: Championed human rights with empathy and understanding.
- Jimmy Carter: Focused on human rights and understanding international issues.
- Ruth Bader Ginsburg: Advocated for gender equality with deep understanding and empathy.
- Magic Johnson: Demonstrated empathy and understanding in his community work.
- Susan Wojcicki: Advocates for diversity and understanding at YouTube.

### Inspirational Voices:
- "The Transformative Power of Classical Music" by Benjamin Zander: Benjamin highlights how understanding and passion can transform experiences and inspire others.

- "The Gift and Power of Emotional Courage" by Susan David: Susan explores the power of emotional courage and understanding in personal and professional growth.
- "Listening to Shame" by Brené Brown: Brené delves into the importance of understanding and addressing shame in building resilience and empathy.
- "The Surprising Science of Happiness" by Dan Gilbert: Dan shares research on happiness, emphasizing the role of understanding our own minds.
- "Want to Change the World? Start by Being Brave Enough to Care" by Cleo Wade: Cleo emphasizes the role of empathy and understanding in making a positive impact.

### Be Vulnerable

For me, being vulnerable means exposing the very soul of myself. I share my fears, frustrations, and anger with my team. It helps them understand where I stand in life, what is important to me, and what I care about. It sets the foundation for difficult situations, be it terminations, retrenchments, technology investments, hires, priorities, coaching, or redefinition of mission. While it is incredibly risky, I cannot tell you just how much benefit being honestly vulnerable has yielded me and my team. It has yielded so much trust, love and understanding, caring hands to support, and bravery.

Vulnerable

When you are vulnerable, you step into your true, authentic self and let your team see the real you, warts and all. You embrace openness and honesty, underpinned by transparency. You let down those self-protective walls even when it feels uncomfortable or risky; it is about sharing your thoughts and feelings in an open, loving way. You acknowledge your own limitations and mistakes while being incredibly open to feedback and saying, "I need a hand with this." Vulnerability is all about owning up to your humanity and taking a chance with other humans.

A controversial subject . . . "Isn't vulnerability too exposing?" It can feel like you are putting your heart on the line, making you open to hurt. It takes guts and a whole lot of self-awareness to be vulnerable. There will be an asshole or two in your life who will go out of their way to weaponize your vulnerability. You have a choice to live your life like it is going to happen tomorrow or live your life like it will happen with two or three people in your workplace environment over the period you work at your company. You get to decide.

That said, you connect with others on a deeper, more authentic level as an invitation to personal growth. You let your guard down and trust others, being open and honest about your experiences. In doing so, you learn and grow stronger. Being vulnerable is a fantastic strength; it demonstrates incredible self-awareness and confidence.

You embrace vulnerability, showing the world your true self and being okay with your imperfections. This leads to incredibly deep and intimate heartfelt connections, resulting in a life that is deeply fulfilling. You are genuine and authentic, transforming your personal and professional relationships.

It fosters deep trust and understanding among team members when they share their vulnerabilities and feelings with you. Vulnerability paves the way for a more authentic, connected team, which leads to better and deeper communication and collaboration.

Choosing to be vulnerable is a personal decision and should be handled with care. It can strengthen relationships and spark personal growth, but it does come with risks. It's crucial to understand your comfort level and set boundaries. Building trust within your team is key to creating a safe space for vulnerability to thrive.

You elevate your effectiveness and the overall health of your company and foster a culture of openness where team members feel safe to express themselves. This trust and openness lead to greater collaboration and innovation. You inspire loyalty and commitment.

Benefits you will experience by being vulnerable include enhanced trust and dedication. You will developer deep, strong relationships that will stand the test of time and stress. You will experience increased engagement, caring and love, and a significant amount of innovation.

Some challenges you will experience include a strong perception of weakness and the risk of being misunderstood or being manipulative. You will have to balance a range of dynamics. You will need to address cultural barriers and face a significant amount of personal discomfort and exposure. It is inevitable that someone will betray you—you need to decide if you will live in fear of that betrayal to revel in the freedom and enrichment of vulnerability.

Some practical steps you can take to become vulnerable include sharing your story, practicing empathy, and encouraging others. You will drive greater innovation and the baseline for what it means to be human—and others will follow. Collective vulnerability is incontestable.

### Ideas to Demonstrate or Inspire:
- *Storytelling sessions*: Organize regular storytelling sessions where team members share personal stories and experiences.
- *Open forums*: Create open forums for discussing challenges and brainstorming solutions.
- *Feedback circles*: Implement feedback circles where everyone, including leaders, gives and receives constructive feedback.
- *Mentorship programs*: Establish mentorship programs that encourage open sharing of experiences and challenges.
- *Mental health days*: Introduce mental health days and encourage team members to take time off when needed.
- *Team-building activities*: Plan activities that promote trust and openness among team members.
- *Anonymous suggestion boxes*: Provide anonymous suggestion boxes for team members to share their thoughts and concerns.

### Authentic People:
- Nelson Mandela: Demonstrated vulnerability by sharing his struggles and advocating for forgiveness.
- Michael Phelps: Open about his struggles with mental health.
- Andre Agassi: Open about his struggles with drug addiction and personal life.

- Marissa Mayer: Known for her openness about professional challenges.
- Ryan Reynolds: Open about his struggles with anxiety.
- Demi Lovato: Vocal about her mental health and addiction struggles.
- Jim Carrey: Shares his mental health struggles and personal challenges.

Inspirational Voices:
- "The Power of Vulnerability" by Brené Brown: Brené explores the importance of vulnerability in leadership, highlighting how it fosters connection and authenticity.
- "Why Good Leaders Make You Feel Safe" by Simon Sinek: Simon discusses the role of empathy and vulnerability in creating a secure and motivated team environment.
- "Get Comfortable with Being Uncomfortable" by Luvvie Ajayi Jones: Luvvie encourages leaders to embrace discomfort and vulnerability to drive change.
- "We're All Hiding Something. Let's Find the Courage to Open Up" by Ash Beckham: Ash advocates for openness and vulnerability in personal and professional relationships.
- "As Work Gets More Complex, 6 Rules to Simplify" by Yves Morieux: Yves emphasizes the importance of vulnerability in navigating workplace complexity.

*"A leader is best when people barely know he exists. When his work is done, his aim fulfilled, they will say: we did it ourselves."*

—**LAO TZU**

# HOW I MADE THESE REAL

Okay, so all of these look like a tall order, but I believe that people who care about people will work with people effectively to find solutions and answers. For those to whom this does not come naturally, attaining some, let alone all, of these will be daunting.

I use these rules as ways of life, which means I apply them to my family, my parents, my siblings, my team, my peers, my leaders and their leaders, and my clients and their clients—in fact, almost everyone I meet for almost any situation. Being human, I fall down regularly, but I always remember, it is not the act of falling or why you fall people will remember; it is the grace with which you get back up that people will not forget. As a leader, you are not alone. You have people around you who will rally with you as you demonstrate your intent to create a safe, healthy space.

The following are some of the ways I have lived inside these guidelines. I implore you to find your match in those that most naturally come to you, and work with those close to you—build your team around you to fill in the gaps of those characteristics that do not naturally match you.

### Apologetic

I am extremely apologetic. I have no hesitation in offering an apology, regardless. I believe that the quicker we can truthfully apologize and accept a situation for what it is, the sooner we can band together to find solutions. I hold myself to very high standards, and when I misstep, say something foolish, or make a mistake, no one holds me more accountable than I do.

Apologizing for situations, actions, and statements helps those around us refocus away from blame and redirect their energy toward resolution. This approach prevents the playing of games, the fire of political discourse, and the weaponization of situations. As a leader, I understand that I own my team's actions, regardless of intent, and I am responsible for creating a harmonious working environment. When we make a mistake, the first thing I do is own it, then apologize, and immediately work to rectify the situation. This creates a solid foundation of integrity and accountability.

It's very important that rapid apologies are followed by reflective changes in behavior or activities. Remember, simply apologizing to make the noise go away is useless; without genuine change, the apology loses its value.

### Authentic

I am always my authentic self, no matter the setting or company. The person you meet is the same person I am with my family, whether we are out hiking, attending a sports or music event; at work; in front of the CEO; and with the newest team member. My consistent authenticity stems from my life experiences that have shaped me. These experiences have taught me to embrace and present my true self in every situation.

My authenticity, combined with other behaviors, often creates a perception of extreme altruism. Many people initially see this as too good to be true. However, as they observe me over time—often months or even a full year—these same people come to understand that my behavior and intent are genuine.

Being authentic means that I don't put on different masks for different occasions. My values and principles remain constant whether I'm interacting with family, friends, colleagues, or leaders. This consistency builds trust and demonstrates integrity.

In professional settings, this means I bring the same level of honesty and dedication to all interactions, fostering a culture of transparency and reliability. In personal settings, it means my family and friends can always count on me to be the same person they know and trust.

By remaining authentic, I build deeper, more meaningful connections with those around me. This approach might seem unusual at first, but it ultimately fosters strong, trusting relationships based on genuine understanding and respect.

## Available

I am always available. While I have scheduled meetings with each of my direct and indirect reports, being accessible on the spot is one of the most crucial ways to show my team that I have their back. Yes, I am available to anyone on my team 24/7, 365 days a year. I have found that random five-minute calls often have a greater impact on my team members' lives and decisions than regular meetings.

My teams have used this access wisely, and it has not once intruded on my personal life or disrupted my work-life balance. The message to my team is clear: I am available whenever and for anything. At no point should they let angst, frustration, or annoyance build up. This constant availability reinforces that I am dependable, responsive, and hold them in high regard. They matter, and they are important.

## Aware

This falls into the category of small but significant things. As a leader, I am keenly aware of my team's workload, busyness, and long hours. I continuously challenge them on why they might be working on a task over the weekend, as I am attentive to their work patterns. I am also mindful of their human interactions, recognizing when they feel they are winning or losing. I adjust my intensity accordingly as I observe them.

Being aware, for me, means noticing the little things: absent smiles, drooping eyes, waning energy, and missed meetings. While I can't be omnipresent, I foster an environment of intense team dynamics where everyone is aware of each other's well-being. We continuously support one another with kind words, hugs, and nudges as needed.

Crossing into their personal world, I remain aware of their home life without intruding into unwelcome space. This holistic awareness helps create a supportive and understanding team environment.

### Brave

This is an important trait because, as leaders, we have to lead, and effective leadership is always pressing for better outcomes. At one of the companies I worked for, there was a tightly bonded team of seventeen people who were not in my reporting line. This team felt ostracized, ignored, overworked, unheard, and unappreciated. I tried to gain their trust for nearly three years, offer support, and be a champion for them, and I failed miserably.

One day I learned that they were blaming me entirely for their difficulties. As usual, I faced the issue head-on and said, "Into the lion's den we go." I'll spare the details, but the team criticized me harshly for decisions, inaction, delays, lack of transparency, and more, none of which I was directly responsible for. They needed someone to vent their frustrations on, and I accepted that role. I wasn't fully aware of their challenges, but this bold step opened a small crack of light for them. Today, the most vocal critic from that meeting has become the team's strongest and most reliable advocate.

That was an extreme example that could have gone completely wrong, which in some ways, it did. However, it led to the team realizing that things aren't always as they seem and that initial awareness is crucial for fostering introspection.

On a lighter note, they say one should not work with family members, but I took another risk and brought in my brother's daughter. This could have gone wrong, too—in fact, I had to let her go years later as we downsized. Despite that, we found it challenging to function effectively without each other. She likely saved the company over a million dollars during our growth phase, and now she's eager to come back while at the same time opening her own company.

## Clear

One of my strengths can also be a challenge: I often communicate through stories. This means I have to make an extra effort to ensure my team understands me and to encourage them to call me out if I start to ramble. While continuously working on this, I strive to provide my team with clear, explicit work instructions, requests, and expectations. I quickly learned that the language I use may not always be clear to others. As the communicator, it is my responsibility to ensure that the person I am speaking to understands my message.

When it comes to work behavior and social contracts, I am explicitly clear. I define straightforward rules, scopes, and engagements. Here are three social contracts I have established with my team:

1. Own everything you do; don't point fingers.
2. Never let me get caught off guard. If I am going to protect, support, and quarterback for you, I need to be fully informed before the game starts.
3. If you are planning to leave, give your team members and peers six months' notice out of respect for them.

These guidelines help create a transparent and accountable work environment.

## Confident

I am confident in who I am and comfortable in my own skin. Over time, I have learned that team members desire leadership, leaders appreciate reliable team members, and companies need people who treat the company as their own.

Through my diverse experiences across various regions, jobs, industries, titles, and cultures, I've discovered that if I need to make ten decisions, eight of them will be spot-on thanks to intuition, gut feeling, and experience. One decision will be somewhat correct, and one will be completely wrong. I have learned to trust my experience-based instincts and am comfortable with the possibility of being wrong, accepting the consequences, and working to resolve any issues. This approach allows me to be highly productive.

My confidence has deep roots in my childhood experiences. From infancy, my mother held me accountable for engaging with my plastic surgeon and medical teams. To provide context, I had a giant nevus on my face, essentially a very hairy birthmark. In 1973, skin grafting and transplantations were still novel concepts—experiments, at best. The process of removing the mark took sixteen years. During this time, two critical experiences shaped my confidence.

Firstly, whenever I entered a room, people often reacted negatively, seeing me as different. I had to learn to be confident in these settings, to understand who I was, and to be comfortable with my situation. Secondly, my mother encouraged me to engage in dialogue with the doctors, to challenge them, and to ask questions before and after each operation. This taught me at a very young age to trust myself and understand that people are just people, regardless of their reactions or titles.

### Consistent

Another important behavior—my team knows how I will behave at any point. It does not matter whether we are joking around or the world is about to collapse. I am consistent in my tenor and tone, in how I listen, react, and respond; I work hard not to surprise my team. This was hard to start with, as the team was always waiting for the outburst, the overreact. It took months for the team to realize that no matter what they bring me or how delicate the situation is, I will always react within the same boundaries.

We always talk about what happened, and then I ask what they need from me, how I can help rectify. Do they need me involved? Do I need to quarterback anything? Where I do overstep or react and either they catch me, or I catch myself, I am wicked quick to apologize.

### Deliberate

Everything I do is driven by action and purpose. I struggle with small talk and idle activities in work, hobbies, or personal connection. I don't have the skill to drift around topics, actions, decisions, or work domains. I am focused on executing and getting things done according to the mission.

This behavior extends to all aspects of my personal life as well. As Yoda says, "Do or do not; there is no try." Sometimes, this intensity catches me off guard, and I come across as too deliberate in light-hearted situations, leading to awkward moments.

Being deliberate helps people around me know that when I get into something, it is mission orientated, always, and yields the appropriate level of engagement.

I don't take on tasks just for the sake of it. I don't complete paperwork just to do it, nor do I draft emails just because. When I get involved, I do it fully and immediately.

We play hard after we have worked hard and got the job done.

## Empathetic

I always put myself in the shoes of the person I am engaging with. I can do this without absorbing their energies, having learned to compartmentalize life and emotions. This allows me to experience situations intensely without letting emotions spill over into other areas. While I understand that their situation is not mine, I can still reflect with them, listen, and see the world from their perspective. As a leader, it is crucial to stay grounded while being fair to all parties involved.

I pay careful attention to my team's interactions—the words they use, their jokes, and even the punctuation in their casual conversations. I take the time to get to know each team member on an intimate level. I also encourage others to support one another in areas where I may lack expertise, creating a multi-layered network of support so the team doesn't rely solely on me.

I believe my intense empathy stems from a deep state of caring—I genuinely care for people. This quality is both my strength and my weakness.

## Fair

If there's one thing I hope to be remembered for, it's that I was always fair. As a company advocate, I work tirelessly to ensure fairness. To me, being fair means setting clear rules and applying them consistently so that no one benefits unfairly, as a golden child or rebel. These rules must be equitable, human, and suitable for the current culture and needs of the company, which means they must constantly evolve.

It can be challenging when individuals face unique situations or are in vulnerable states, whether personally or professionally. Balancing fairness with empathy and compassion can sometimes conflict with established rules and precedents. Whether it's about time off, promotions, adopting new technologies, bereavement, salary increases, workload, or project participation, I strive to find a balance.

This often means adjusting the rules based on the individual's experiences, contributions, and challenges. It's important to ensure that these adjustments do not create new precedents that could harm others.

### Gentle

We are dealing with humans. Every human is where they are from the sum of life, none of which any of us know anything about. I am consciously and exceedingly gentle in the words I use and the way I engage all topics. I am quite firm and directive, but in a way that sees the human for who they are, right then in the moment.

I see each person for whom they allow themselves to be seen as all the time. I match engagement styles and yield to being gentle and compassionate all the time.

An example of being firm, fair, and gentle is as follows: I had a team member whose mother was diagnosed as terminal and wanted to go full distant remote. (I don't subscribe to full remote—see below.) I asked if this was going to be a temporary or permanent move, and she said permanent. I was incredibly human, gentle, and firm in telling her she needed to go to her mother, period.

At the same time, I told her that it is my experience that people in a highly intense environment which is technically volatile (as we were) would within six to nine months either self-eject or be ejected by the team through perceived non-participation. This was not to scare her away, pressure, or coerce any decision or outcome. It was in the spirit of open, honest, informed, caring discussions. She knows I will support her no matter what.

Being gentle and human does not mean mothering people, being submissive, or being overly yielding. It just means being gentle with your words, approach, body language, and support while being firm.

## Graceful

I recognize life is tough. I hold myself to a very high standard in many aspects of life, much higher than anyone around me could try. I have to keep reminding myself to give myself grace.

Working with my team while pushing deliberately with persistence, it is inevitable that people will fail and hold themselves to a higher standard than I would. I am continuously reminding them to give themselves grace and space to fail. Same with team members that appear not to be rowing in the same direction—I implore my team to help course correct that person whether they are on our team or not, and to be graceful as they do it, using caring words and approaches.

Life in general is hard, and I don't believe people innately behave as assholes intentionally. We are all dealing with stuff, trying to muddle through life, and we all take a step into asshole mode without realizing the consequences. It is so important to help the person become aware, and then give the person the grace and space to recover. As a rule, I give the person the benefit of the doubt and encourage my team members to do the same.

## Human

I see every person for the individual they are. I acknowledge and appreciate the unique qualities, characteristics, and experiences that make each person who they are. I avoid generalizations and stereotypes, recognizing that everyone has a unique story and perspective. I refrain from imposing personal biases, expectations, or predefined notions based on roles, appearances, or assumptions. I allow each person to present who and what they are.

I take time to get to know people and engage with them as they are. I Invest effort in understanding and interacting with people on a deeper, more authentic level. This involves active listening, open-mindedness, and a willingness to learn about others without judgment.

I accept and respect people as they are by embracing and honoring individuals for their true selves, without trying to change or mold them to fit any personal standards or expectations.

I continuously seek to understand people's evolving identities, experiences, and viewpoints. This approach involves ongoing curiosity and adaptability in relationships, recognizing that people grow and change over time. I choose to see every person and engage with them as they are and consciously interact with people in their most genuine form through authentic, meaningful connections.

### Intentional

When I engage with others, I am fully present. While my mind is constantly considering various dimensions, my focus is entirely on the moment at hand. Eye contact is crucial; I make sure to look at the person I'm engaging with. I lean in with an open posture, making it clear that I am attentive and that I care.

I collaborate with my team to set specific and clear objectives, guiding them to identify their own goals and helping them develop their own roadmaps. When I attend meetings, it is with a clear purpose.

I am committed to continuously learning about leadership, constantly seeking new methods, approaches, and dialogues to navigate our ever-evolving society. I strive to be intentional in all my actions, avoiding accidental decisions and ensuring that everything I do is purposeful.

### Interested

I tend to stay unengaged, not uninterested, in the daily work activities of my team members. If they need my input, they will reach out, and I am ready to dive deep into the topic.

However, I am profoundly interested in them as individuals. I want to understand their thought processes, decision-making, reasons for action and inaction, motivations, career aspirations, and attitudes toward autonomy and micromanagement. I am also curious about their personal lives, including their families, hobbies, and passions.

I invest time in getting to know them personally, engaging with them when invited into their family lives. I make myself available for dinners at their homes, spending time with their significant others and children. We share a glass of wine and immerse ourselves in their world. I cherish this precious time and make an effort to experience it fully. When traveling between offices, this has included multiple breakfasts, lunches, dinners, and evening events with different team members.

This personal investment is evident to all team members, whether they report to me or not. Spending this time with them helps me learn about the core of who they are, enriching my understanding of their work skills and creating a well-rounded view of each person.

The key is being invited in—while you can involve yourself in work events and activities, entering someone's personal world requires an invitation. I never take these invitations for granted.

### Inspirational

I have a natural talent in the area of inspiration. I have a natural wealth of energy by not allowing things to get to me, and I allow myself to experience extreme highs and lows. I harness the energies and love for life and engage with vigor, all the time. I inspire and guide by truly understanding the individual: their actions, their thought processes, their strengths, and areas where they struggle. I focus on both their remarkable abilities and the areas they tend to avoid, recognizing the hidden potential they may not see or may be afraid to explore. I connect these behaviors to their goals, outcomes, and desires, challenging them to grow, take risks, and be ambitious. I achieve this through small questions and gentle nudges, asking why not and what's stopping them.

It does help that I have a never-ending supply of energy, passion, and love for people and life.

I also offer pro bono mentorship. At one event, I had the privilege of speaking with a gentleman in his mid-twenties seeking a job change. He was eager for a change and was *waiting* for something to find him. I asked him why he was waiting and if he was happy with his current job and learning opportunities. He admitted he was not. During our twenty-minute conversation, he revealed that he was Chinese, living in Atlanta, and wanted to move to Japan to start his own UI/UX company in six years. We concluded with a clear set of steps for him to follow. He realized that he could either actively pursue his dreams or passively wait for luck while continuing to serve someone else. He walked away with a mission to execute.

Inspiring someone is straightforward: listen, care, be honest, and ask, "Why? Why not? What does it look like?"

### Kind

Amidst the challenges we all have, I strive to be an exception in my interactions with people, consistently going the extra mile to connect with and recognize the humanity in each person. My goal is to truly see them for who they are and find meaningful ways to appreciate and acknowledge them. I am mindful of words, phrases, and situations I put people in, especially when missteps happen.

Being kind is simple: just work to not be the accidental asshole. It's important to shift the focus away from yourself and stop trying to one-up others. Let others have their moment, whether it's taking the last piece of cake or choosing the last color—small acts of kindness can be incredibly impactful. By putting others first in these small ways, we can create moments of joy and appreciation that they may not often experience.

People already have enough to deal with. Life is hard, and everyone carries their own burdens. Being kind respects the human. It creates a level playing field to engage with people, removes unintended hostilities, and neutralizes situations.

### Loved

I allow myself to be loved. I recognize and celebrate the love that others give me. This is incredibly challenging for me because I struggle deeply with accepting help and acts of kindness from others—it feels almost like an allergic reaction. Love often comes with acts of devotion and care and people going out of their way for you, and I find this difficult to accept. While I am comfortable giving love and support, receiving it is hard to describe. Nonetheless, I make a conscious effort to embrace it and celebrate these moments with my team. My team (at writing) will not yield to me avoiding being loved. They often go out of their way to drive this home in unavoidable ways.

## Loving

I love freely and openly. I share my love with my family, friends, hobbies, and the complex life I've created for myself. I love working hard and seeing people succeed. I love serving others. I love the Minions. I love my Christmas light display with forty-five thousand lights on my house. I love working with wood and building furniture. I love my team.

I cherish the fact that my team feels so connected to the things I love that they participate in some of them and have embraced these passions as their own. When it comes to the Minions, they've taken almost complete ownership, creating drawings and paintings and giving thoughtful gifts like coffee mugs, daily self-guidebooks with Minion quotes and words of wisdom, toys, and cards.

## Open-Minded

I am stoic in my ways, maintaining a calm and steadfast demeanor. I tend to be outspoken and often speak more than I should. I am opinionated and firm in my beliefs. If I have done something well and successfully for over ten years, I believe my way is the best, period—that is until someone demonstrates a better approach. When they do, I pivot immediately.

I strive to balance my perspectives by seeking a yin to my yang in all topics. This is because I recognize my tendency to be stubborn and dogmatic, especially when dealing with people who seem to have alternate agendas. I genuinely appreciate it when my direct reports challenge me on concepts, regardless of the topic. Creating safe spaces for open-minded thinking allows me to be receptive to new ideas while maintaining a healthy level of resistance because I understand their heart and intent.

Having people challenge my views and ideas is a humbling and growing experience. It helps me and the team evolve. It fosters an environment of mutual respect and continuous improvement. By encouraging diverse viewpoints and being open to change, I aim to lead with both conviction and flexibility, always ready to learn and adapt for the betterment of the team and our goals.

I apply this to all parts of life, but focusing on work, I try to be open-minded about how I lead and address topics, what to address when, how to go about solving problems, what solutions should be applied, and who to include.

### Passionate

I love life, and this topic is one of the most important, rewarding, and revealing aspects of who I am. I live by a simple rule: work hard, play hard. This doesn't necessarily mean equal time spent on work and play, but rather a balance that brings a sense of fulfillment and completeness. My mother ingrained in me that life is for the living. Life experiences and values won't come to me; I must actively seek them out every day.

I am passionate about life and people. The old saying, "Do something you love, and you won't work a day in your life," resonates deeply with me. I am exuberantly passionate about helping others find their footing, become self-aware, and drive toward success. I often do this at the expense of my career, scope, responsibilities, and finances—and I am perfectly okay with that.

My childhood taught me that there can always be more serious challenges than the ones we face at that moment. From those experiences, I learned to generate my own energy. Every morning, I wake up and choose to be passionate and engaged. There is no magic blue or red pill; it's a conscious decision. As the quote from *Shawshank Redemption* goes, "Get busy living, or get busy dying." I choose to live on the edge of passion every day. If you can't find that passion with the people around you or in your job, change it!

I am passionate about my interests outside of work, and I love sharing these passions with my team. Whether it's my fascination with Minions, woodworking, decorating my house with forty-five thousand Christmas lights, or celebrating a team member's success, like a life event, a project, or a race won, I bring the same enthusiasm and joy to these activities as I do to my work.

Living life to its fullest means embracing every moment, every opportunity, and every challenge with open arms. It's about creating a life that is rich with experiences, connections, and achievements that go beyond the professional sphere. It's about finding joy in both the grand adventures and the simple pleasures and sharing that joy with those around you.

## Patient (Patience)

This virtue is a peculiar one for me. I have no patience for teaching my mom or wife how to use Excel. I have no tolerance for obtuse, obstructive, or bullying behavior. However, I have all the time in the world for someone who genuinely wants to change themselves, their lives, and their trajectories.

When working with anyone who shows the desire and determination to change, patience is essential—often like a pinch of salt. I relish the process of probing to see if someone has discovered their inner strength or voice. I enjoy challenging them to take the next growth step, whether it's through a Zoom session or coffee meeting or by confronting something they thought was impossible. As a leader, it is my responsibility to recognize when someone is ready for the next step. I own this process and give them the space and time to reach those milestones where ongoing growth becomes inevitable.

This often means waiting months, or even years, for someone to open their eyes, overcome their fear of missing out (FOMO), realize they don't need to do everything themselves, learn effective communication, and figure out how to manage interactions with the CEO or their peers. Patience in this context is critical, as it allows individuals to develop at their own pace and achieve lasting personal and professional growth.

## Persistent (Persistence)

My determination, while a strength, can sometimes lead to being overly persistent: the dog that caught the tire. I am driven by cause and mission, and I do not let up. This tenacity is beneficial when working with the team, driving toward execution, and maintaining relentless focus. However, it can become overwhelming when holding people to high standards with a relentless push to keep doing more.

I recognize that I can be a bit too persistent: my team helps me remain aware. When they raise concerns, we talk about it—why I am pressing and the reasons behind my persistence. As leaders, we must lead by example, ensuring that work is not treated like a party. We work hard, and the celebration starts once the work is done. This principle applies to everyone I engage with, personal and professional.

### Predictable

No matter what is happening, who is involved, or the situation I find myself in, my reactions are consistent within the boundaries of my relationship with the person I am engaged with. I vary my levels of intensity and transparency based on the key stakeholders and team members I am interacting with. This means that some people experience more intensity, forward thinking, and brainstorming from me than others. While my goal is to engage with everyone uniformly, I recognize that some people mature and adapt to fluidity, high change, and unknowns faster than others, while others excel at handling interpersonal dynamics and day-to-day challenges.

Each of these relationships has its own style of engagement, and I remain completely predictable within these. If I am ever off balance, my team members know they can approach me, as they understand my predictability, to highlight any discrepancies.

I have team members who have asked for one-on-ones following decisions or meetings where it was clear to them that I was not engaging as expected. They have done this with compassion and love. They have walked me through engagement they observed was not aligned to the core of me—some knowingly and some unknowingly. This has ranged from leadership misalignment to hiring decisions and reprimands that are due, or not.

This opens up a conversation about what might be going on and why, allowing us to address any issues together.

### Present

I am always absolutely present with the person I am engaged with—unless I am on a video call, and then multi-tasking steps in. While I am very good at very rapid context switching (multi-tasking), I acknowledge this to be disrespectful. I work hard to try to have both hands in view on the camera.

When I am with people, the phone goes away, and I try to remove any desks or obstacles that create perceived walls between people that allow me to be here in the moment. I look for situations that remove distractions and tell the person, "I am here with you, and it is just us."

I actively listen by paraphrasing what is shared with me and discussing topics in a way that is appropriate to the moment and the person I am speaking with. I work to make sure the person feels and experiences being heard. This approach requires mindfulness of the relationship and sensitivity to the topic at hand.

### Purposeful

Nearly everything I do has a purpose (and is deliberate), unless it's about playing hard—well, even that is purposeful. This purposefulness is beneficial when driving tasks to completion and when the team needs a push or closure. However, for the person on the receiving end, it can be daunting because I don't yield easily. This approach can create challenges with peers that I need to address.

My team knows that when it's time to work, it's time to work. The office is not a place for games or filling the day with unnecessary activities—until the work is done. I avoid booking hour-long meetings; my default is thirty minutes. Every meeting is as short as possible, focused on discussing the topic, making decisions, sharing information, and then ending the meeting. If someone is part of a project, they are there for a reason, and if they're not engaged, they should excuse themselves. Power meetings are vital; I am intentional in bringing people together and directing them to get back to their tasks.

I am aware that this can be painful for others. However, being purposeful is essential because wasting time is the costliest mistake we can make.

### A Servant

I Serve!

I tell my teams that we are servant-leaders, as we are operations. No one will thank us when everything runs smoothly, on time, and without issues. However, they will be quick to blame operations if anything goes wrong. No matter, we are servants; leaders are servants first and foremost.

I serve the CEO by always being available, keeping them informed, taking on tasks they shouldn't be bogged down with, and responding immediately to their needs.

I serve my peers by handling tasks that don't utilize their strengths in driving the company forward. I consolidate information, filter out the noise, and provide insights that help them prioritize and deliver results. I respond promptly, regardless of the time or day.

I serve my leaders by removing obstacles from their path. I take on menial tasks that don't leverage their skills, making myself available to listen and assist with whatever they need to get their work done.

I serve my indirect reports by hearing them, being available for them, being an ear for them.

I coach my teams to serve with a smile, engage with the person they are working with in the way they need them to, accept that being a servant is thankless, and recognize and look after other servants.

I serve the company by always being switched on, ensuring fairness, giving everyone a voice, and making sure everyone has what they need.

I am a servant.

### Sincere

It's challenging to talk about how I have implemented this, but it boils down to executing many principles discussed in this section of the book. I always mean what I say and say what I mean. I don't engage in wordplay or life games. I encourage discourse, active debate, and open discussion. I urge my team to challenge me and strive to remain open and honest at all times. When I can't answer a question for any reason, I am upfront about it.

I do not respond with what I think people want to hear. I engage sincerely at all levels of relationships, always meaning what I say and caring deeply about what is communicated. I engage with intense caring and commitment to genuine interactions.

## Transparent

Certain topics and information belong within specific domains or groups of people. Within the appropriate domains, I err on the side of oversharing. I do this thoughtfully, considering my team members' readiness to handle the information. For instance, one team member once asked, "If you know where we need to be, why don't you just tell us so we can get there quickly?" My response was that not everyone is ready for the information or the vision of our future. Some people, upon knowing the destination, might even work against it, both overtly and covertly.

I promote transparency as much as possible without compromising individuals or the organization. This inevitably creates some tough discussions. I am not a supporter of information hoarding, or the weaponization thereof. I am a strong believer that given the larger context and, where appropriate (more often than not), the details, people feel like they know what is happening.

I recognize that some people cannot handle details and others need details. I am very mindful of the level of insights shared with whom, at what stage.

I conduct a weekly executive committee briefing where I cover the high-level topics discussed by the executive team. I highlight specific issues that might impact my team and encourage them to seek out the details, contribute where they can, and take necessary actions.

Additionally, I share general insights on investments, executive discussions, and conflict resolution, especially if there are known misalignments. My team is always aware of the company's ebbs and flows, priorities, and discussion topics. This knowledge is vital for them to feel like they truly belong to the company.

### Understanding

I recognize that none of us is perfect. We all have flaws and limitations, and it's essential to approach every interaction with empathy and patience, knowing everyone is doing their best despite imperfections.

I strive to understand how people think by delving into their thought processes, which helps me communicate effectively and build trust. Acknowledging everyone's hard work creates a supportive environment and empowers and motivates others.

Some individuals consistently push the extra mile, driving progress and inspiring others. Supporting their efforts ensures they remain motivated and continue to excel. I consider the entirety of a person's background, skills, and character, ensuring fair and holistic assessments.

Understanding that heart and intent drive behavior helps me respond compassionately, resolving conflicts and fostering a supportive environment. Mistakes are inevitable, and treating them as learning opportunities encourages growth and innovation without fear of judgment.

People desire leadership, seeking guidance from someone they trust and respect. Providing clear vision, support, and encouragement helps others reach their potential and contribute meaningfully to our collective goals.

### Vulnerable

I tend to err on the side of complete vulnerability. This approach has burned me a few times. The value I've gained far exceeds the setbacks. Being vulnerable means sharing parts of myself that are deeply personal and sometimes uncomfortable. I've openly discussed fears, what makes me angry, and childhood experiences that have shaped my perspectives and defined some of my current positions. I talk about the journey that brought me to where I am today, including what hurts me, what I love, my passions, and my hobbies.

As my relationships with individuals have matured, I've found myself sharing more profound aspects of my life. I discuss my views on love and life, the importance of sanctity and stability, and my personal fears and frustrations. This level of openness is not just about revealing my own vulnerabilities, but rather about fostering a culture of trust and authenticity, creating a platform where my team understands me and my decision structure. This way they learn to decide and execute without me.

By being so open, I've gotten to know my team members very well. This vulnerability has been a gateway to understanding the people I work with on a deeper level. I've learned why they think the way they do, the underlying complexities that drive them, and the factors that shape their behaviors. I understand why they present themselves in certain ways and why they might be hesitant or fearful of taking charge.

This insight is invaluable. It allows me to connect with my team members in a way that goes beyond professional interactions. I can support them better because I understand their motivations, challenges, and fears. They see me as human—just like them—with my own set of challenges and vulnerabilities. This mutual understanding fosters a strong, cohesive team dynamic where everyone feels seen and valued.

By presenting myself as nothing more and nothing less than human, I create an environment where authenticity is encouraged. My team knows that it's okay to be vulnerable, to make mistakes, and to express their true selves. This has led to a culture of openness and trust, where we support each other not just as colleagues but as people who genuinely care for one another.

*"No person will make a great leader who wants to do it all himself, or to get all the credit for doing it."*
—**ANDREW CARNEGIE**

# WORKING WITH YOUR TEAM

This section assumes that you have a solid understanding of who you are and the characteristics you naturally exhibit. Self-awareness is the first step in being an effective leader and allows you to lead with authenticity and confidence. Below, we shift to how you could engage with your team members, as building strong relationships with your team is crucial to fostering a productive and positive work environment.

The intent of this section is to provide you with practical tips on how to work with your team and drive toward success. Leading is understanding the unique dynamics of your team, recognizing individual strengths and weaknesses, and creating an atmosphere where everyone feels valued and motivated.

### Create Leaders

Be a multiplier. Your team and company are dependent on you identifying team members on your team who have leadership abilities. You are responsible for your team's leadership growth along with the development of leaders within your team. This ensures the sustainability of the team and company. These potential leaders will show initiative by being proactive in solving problems, demonstrate strong communication skills, and have a natural ability to influence and motivate others.

Assign them to projects or committees and give them responsibilities and opportunities to lead. Place them into a position that will force their hand and allow them to experiment and develop leadership insights and capabilities in practical settings. Mentorship is a powerful development tool offering guidance and support through your experiences and insights. You should check in with them regularly to provide feedback and guidance. You are responsible for helping them navigate challenges while building confidence and competence.

This is a continuous journey of learning and growth. Encourage them to pursue development opportunities and provide access to resources (books and online materials) that can help them expand their knowledge and skills. Cultivate a growth mindset, including learning and development through effort and perseverance. Encourage them to embrace challenges and learn from their failures while continuously seeking improvement. A growth mindset fosters resilience and adaptability, which are essential qualities for effective leadership.

Empower your team by giving them the authority to make decisions and take ownership of their tasks. Hold them accountable for performance and provide constructive feedback. Create a sense of ownership and responsibility, driving them to excel in their roles through empowerment and accountability.

Promote a culture where development is valued and encouraged while growth efforts are recognized and rewarded. This ensures that their development becomes an integral part of the company's fabric, leading to continuous improvement and innovation.

Regularly provide specific, actionable feedback highlighting their strengths and areas for improvement. This ongoing dialogue supports their development and helps them become more effective. Celebrate achievements and accomplishments that reinforce positive behaviors, and motivate them to continue striving for excellence.

Pressing your team into growth is essential for building a resilient and high-performing company. Offer mentorship and encourage continuous learning. Foster a growth mindset where you create an environment in which leaders thrive.

## Bring Them Together

It is your responsibility to bring the team together rather than being directly involved in every aspect of their work, you do this by creating an environment where the team can function effectively and cohesively without your constant presence. The goal is for you to become superfluous. This means the team should be able to operate independently and efficiently even when you are not there.

The ultimate measure of your effectiveness as a leader is becoming superfluous. This doesn't mean you are no longer needed, but rather that the team is so well-prepared and capable that they don't rely on you for day-to-day operations. Your role transitions to one of a mentor and strategic guide focusing on the big picture and long-term goals while the team handles the details.

Fostering a sense of unity and collaboration within the team is crucial. This involves creating opportunities for team members to bond and share ideas while working together toward common goals. Facilitate regular formal and informal team-building activities to strengthen relationships and improve communication. Encourage open dialogue and transparency so everyone feels comfortable sharing their thoughts and concerns.

A truly successful team should be able to function smoothly in your absence. This means developing their problem-solving skills, decision-making capabilities, and leadership potential. Delegate responsibilities and empower team members to take ownership of their tasks and projects. Provide them with the necessary resources and guidance. Refrain from micromanaging. Trust them to make decisions and solve problems on their own.

Encourage your team to find and own their collective identity. This involves allowing them to develop their own unique culture and values. Support them in creating norms and practices that reflect their strengths and preferences. By doing so, you help them build a strong, cohesive identity that drives their performance and satisfaction.

It's important to remember that you are part of the team and not the team itself. The team should not exist because of you. It should thrive because of the collective efforts and synergy of its members. By empowering the team to function independently, you ensure its sustainability and resilience. This approach fosters a sense of ownership and pride among team members, leading to higher motivation and engagement while improving productivity.

By working on bringing the team together and fostering their independence, you create a robust and resilient team capable of achieving great results without relying on your constant presence. This approach not only enhances the team's performance and satisfaction but also allows you to focus on strategic leadership and long-term goals. Ultimately, a team that can function effectively without you is a testament to your success as a leader.

## Find Your Evangelists

Finding and empowering your evangelists within the team can significantly amplify your leadership scalability and foster a cohesive, proactive environment. Identify team members who show exceptional enthusiasm and a deep understanding of the team's mission. These individuals should naturally influence others and positively impact team dynamics. Look for those who are highly engaged, supportive team members who display a genuine passion for the work.

Provide these team members with the autonomy and authority to lead initiatives and drive activities or projects. Empowerment boosts confidence and commitment that will equip them with the necessary resources and support to succeed, including information and mentorship. Some will naturally excel and take on additional responsibilities. Identify those who deeply understand and resonate with the team's mission, as they will passionately articulate the mission and inspire others.

Team members who are well-connected with the floor often have valuable insights and feedback. Use their connections to stay informed about team sentiments and issues. They can act as trust ambassadors and bridge the gap between leadership and the broader team. Your evangelists will distribute leadership information and responsibilities, effectively multiplying your capacity to influence the team. Trust them to execute and lead effectively.

Take the time to understand what drives each of your evangelists, including their career aspirations, personal interests, and intrinsic motivations. Use this to tailor your engagement styles with each of them and provide them with responsibilities that align with their motivations and strengths.

Communicate the vision and mission to your evangelists and ensure they understand and are committed to the cause. Involve them in strategic discussions and decision-making processes; their buy-in is crucial for rallying the broader team. Assign ownership of key projects and initiatives and foster a sense of responsibility and accountability. Define expectations and goals clearly and provide them with the autonomy to achieve objectives in their own way. Ensure that your evangelists echo your messaging and values consistently across the team.

Empowered and engaged teams can anticipate and address issues before they escalate. This leads to proactive problem-solving. Foster a culture of continuous improvement to identify and implement solutions independently. These evangelists can significantly amplify your impact in disseminating your vision, foster collaboration, and solve problems ahead of the curve.

### Evangelical Teams

As the team bonds, there is a risk that they will become perceived as a favored group receiving disproportionate attention and resources. Perceptions like this breed resentment and division. It is crucial to avoid this by ensuring that your team remains grounded and inclusive, sharing their successes and methodologies in a quiet, humble way.

Your team should work to hold the high ground all the time. Holding the high ground means maintaining honorable and ethical behavior with a commitment to excellence in all actions. Your team should embody these principles and demonstrate qualities that inspire others.

When your team hears noise on the floor—rumors, complaints, or misunderstandings—they should gently refute it with facts or own it if it's valid. This proactive approach helps maintain transparency and trust within the organization. Encourage your team to address issues head-on, providing clear and honest communication to dispel any misinformation or resolve legitimate concerns.

Organizational politics can be detrimental to team cohesion and productivity. Empower your team to call out political behavior when they see it, promoting a culture of openness and fairness. By addressing favoritism, manipulation, or hidden agendas, you help create a healthier work environment where merit and collaboration are prioritized.

Encourage your team to make their engagement style with you visible to other leaders. This means demonstrating how they communicate, collaborate, and solve problems in a way that sets a positive example. Share their successful strategies and behaviors in cross-departmental meetings and company events. This visibility helps other leaders adopt similar practices.

As a leader, your actions set the tone for the entire team. By embodying the values and behaviors you expect from your team, you lead by example. This approach creates a ripple effect, encouraging others to follow suit. Common sense is viral. When people see practical and collaborative behavior stick, they will likely adopt these practices themselves.

Holding your team accountable for their growth and avoiding the pitfalls of favoritism while promoting a culture of transparency and fairness are key aspects of effective leadership. By making your team's engagement style visible and leading by example, you set the stage for a more cohesive environment.

### Coach Communication

Coaching your team to communicate effectively is fundamental to building a cohesive and high-performing group. This involves guiding them through crucial conversations, helping them become trusted advisors, teaching them about your peers, and teaching them when and how to speak appropriately. Understanding how to decode each other's communication styles and effectively creating business cases are also vital skills. Encourage your team to call each other out respectfully and engage in healthy debate. Navigate disagreement and manage conflict constructively.

This means teaching them how to communicate in a way that the person receiving the message actually hears it, meaning knowing how to decode situations to understand human dynamics and to communicate with intent to be heard and not to say, "I told you so."

Crucial conversations are those that significantly impact relationships and outcomes. Coaching your team on how to handle these discussions with clarity and empathy is essential. It helps them address sensitive topics without escalating tensions and ensures that important issues are resolved effectively. This involves fostering a sense of integrity, competence, and empathy in their interactions. By becoming a trusted advisor and coaching your team in this way, you ensure your team is seen as reliable and insightful by their peers and leaders.

Teaching them about your peers and their communication styles helps your team understand the broader organizational landscape. This knowledge enables them to tailor their communication strategies to different stakeholders, enhancing their influence and effectiveness. Knowing when to speak is equally important; timing can be crucial in getting a message across effectively. Encourage your team to be mindful of the right moments to voice their opinions and concerns.

Decoding one another's communication styles involves understanding the verbal and non-verbal cues that indicate how a message is received and understood. This skill helps in avoiding misunderstandings and ensures that communication is clear and effective. Creating business cases is another critical aspect. Teach your team how to build compelling arguments for their ideas supported by data and aligned with organizational goals. This helps secure buy-in from stakeholders and drives initiatives forward.

Encourage your team to call each other out respectfully when necessary. Constructive feedback and accountability are key to continuous improvement and maintaining high standards. Debate, disagreement, and conflict are natural in any team setting. Coaching your team on how to engage in these interactions productively ensures that they lead to growth and innovation rather than discord.

Effective communication is the bedrock of everything within a team. While it's unrealistic to expect to always get what you want, shared communication opens many doors. It removes a lot of perceptions and breaks down many walls, fostering a more collaborative and understanding environment. By investing in your team's communication skills, you're equipping them with the tools they need to navigate the complexities of the workplace and build stronger relationships in a drive to achieve collective success.

## Create Reasons to Get Together

Events are a powerful tool for fostering team cohesion and building strong interpersonal relationships. These events provide an opportunity for team members to interact outside the work environment, breaking down barriers, building trust, and creating a sense of camaraderie.

Create events exclusively for team members, without partners and children. This allows team members to engage with one another on a personal level without family distractions or obligations. It promotes deeper connections and encourages open communication through team-building exercises and sports activities. Casual outings are highly effective in this context.

Also create events inclusive of partners and children. These family-inclusive events help team members see each other as humans with lives outside of the office. They foster a family-friendly culture and promote understanding while building a supportive community. Picnics and family fun days are excellent events.

Provide opportunities for team members to mix outside of the office, ranging from informal gatherings like happy hours and lunches to more formally structured activities such as sports leagues or book clubs. The key is to offer diverse options that cater to different interests, ensuring everyone feels included and can participate.

Be present at these events and manage your participation thoughtfully. At times, you need to be present for the entire event to show your commitment and support. For other events, leave early and allow the team to bond without feeling like they are under your watchful eye. This keeps you approachable while giving your team the space they need to form their own connections.

Encourage events and participation without you. This autonomy empowers your team to take ownership of their social interactions, gives them a sense of independence, and helps them bond naturally and authentically.

At specific events, make it a point to stay until the end. Your presence shows that you value these moments and the effort your team puts into them. It demonstrates your commitment to team bonding and allows you to experience the dynamics of your team in a relaxed setting. Your goal is to blend in and engage with your team as an equal. This helps in building trust and respect.

The primary goal of organizing these events is to create as many non-work-related bonding opportunities as possible. These interactions build stronger relationships that translate into better teamwork and collaboration.

Examples of events include a softball league, soccer matches, bowling nights, board game nights, trivia nights, video game tournaments, milestone celebrations, holidays, and company achievements with themed parties. To provide a relaxed atmosphere for socializing, arrange regular happy hours, BBQs, potluck dinners, and outings to concerts, theater performances, or art exhibitions. Break the normal routine.

Remember that not all team members will like or attend all of the events. Change them up and expect mixed participation. Facilitate participation and create a platform for people to be larger than the work they do.

By organizing a variety of events, you create numerous opportunities for your team to bond outside of work. These interactions foster a sense of community and build stronger relationships while enhancing overall team cohesion. Your presence and participation in these events show your commitment to building a positive and supportive team culture.

## Culture Creation

Drawing your evangelists into the process of culture creation is essential to fostering a cohesive and engaging environment. Your evangelists are the cultural core you are building. They embody and promote the values and behaviors throughout the organization.

Your evangelists promote and amplify your culture, consistently demonstrating the values and behaviors agreed to be the norm. This sets the tone for the balance of the team, who will reinforce the culture.

Engage your evangelists and keep them motivated and aligned with your cultural vision. Organize events inside and outside office hours to foster a sense of community and shared purpose. These activities can include team-building events referred to above. By driving different types of activities, you help form stronger connections and deepen commitments to the cultural goals.

The culture of a company is fundamental to its identity and success. It is larger than any single person and serves as the backbone that can either attract or repel talent. A strong positive culture creates an environment where team members feel valued and motivated to contribute their best. A toxic culture can lead to high turnover and low morale, resulting in decreased productivity.

Consider implementing initiatives such as the following:

- *Newsletter*: This could highlight cultural achievements and recognize individual and team contributions, with important updates.
- *Website*: Have a dedicated section that showcases the culture, values, and mission, reinforcing while communicating externally.
- *Culture deck*: This tool outlines the company's values, expectations, and behaviors, serving as a reference for team and new hires.

By drawing your evangelists into the process of culture creation, you leverage their influence and enthusiasm to build a strong and cohesive environment. Their active involvement ensures the culture becomes a living, breathing aspect of the organization, driving engagement, productivity, and long-term success.

## Keep Your Team Informed

Keeping your team informed about the broader context in which they operate is crucial for alignment and motivation. Hold regular group meetings to update them on relevant changes in strategy and priorities, keeping them in the know of how their work fits into the bigger picture. The key is being able to help your team step back from the moving parts they are within and to help them see the wholistic picture of all the moving parts around them. Be transparent about challenges that might affect the team, ensuring your team members are not caught off guard by unexpected developments.

Provide context for decisions and changes. Help your team understand why certain decisions are made and how they impact overall goals and objectives. Clarify priorities to help them focus on what matters by clearly defining and communicating, ensuring everyone understands the key objectives and their rationale.

Help team members see how their individual tasks and projects align with broader team and company goals. This connection highlights the importance of their work and keeps them motivated. Periodically reassess and adjust priorities as necessary. The business environment can change rapidly, and keeping the team updated on shifting priorities is critical.

You need to decide just what information you share with them. Keep in mind that what you share with them today versus what you can share with them after eighteen months of growth and development will change. You must continuously evaluate what you share with them and trust they will not leverage the information you share and distribute news without your say-so.

You will find there are team members you can talk to about the inevitable shutdown of the company and others whom you cannot even mention a change in leave policy is imminent. Be smart about who you engage with. Finding team members who you can engage veraciously with can help bring a different view or solution to problems you and your peers have been muddled by to no end and no outcome. Be smart—never condone or facilitate the weaponization of knowledge or insights.

## Give Them Agency

Empowering your team with agency means giving them the authority, autonomy, and resources to make decisions and take actions independently. This approach involves trusting your team members to use their skills and judgment to contribute to the organization's success without needing constant supervision or approval.

Allow team members to make decisions within their scope of work and trust they will handle their responsibilities. Do not micromanage. Allow them the authority to influence their projects' outcomes.

Ensure your team has access to the necessary tools and resources, including training. This may include finances, time, software, equipment, or development opportunities. While giving autonomy, offer guidance and support when needed, being ever mindful that you are trying to help them build scale muscles and mindfully not telling them how the mission is to be delivered. Be available for questions and advice.

Create an environment where they feel safe to experiment, innovate, and take calculated risks. Encourage them to propose new ideas and solutions and allow room for creative approaches to problem-solving. Encourage team members to take ownership of their projects and tasks. Assign responsibilities that challenge them and align with their skills and career goals.

When team members have agency, they are more motivated and engaged; they feel valued and trusted. Autonomy and the ability to influence one's work leads to higher job satisfaction and reduced turnover. Teams with agency are more likely to innovate and find creative solutions to problems.

By giving your team agency, you empower them to take control of their world, leading to greater innovation, efficiency, and satisfaction.

## Hold Them Accountable

It is essential to hold your team accountable for their growth and development, not just their deliverables. This means you need to encourage them to think and stretch beyond their current capabilities, striving for higher standards and broader perspectives.

Their accountability should extend beyond immediate tasks to include the promotion of the broader mission and values. Encourage them to share knowledge and strategies along with their successes with other teams.

Being autonomous and making one's own decisions is exciting, freeing once the team realizes that this is a reality and that no one is looking over their shoulders. Your team must understand that with this comes accountability. They are responsible for getting the work done and making the decisions.

At the end of the accountability line is you—if your team messes up, it is on you. Between actions and there being a mess, your team must take ownership of what they do and say. Helping them understand the consequences of their actions is critical.

At no stage should your team, for whatever reason, be pointing a finger at someone else for their failures, no excuses! We work, we own, we do, we win, or we fail, and then we work to win again!

Failure does not only mean one team member's product is broken or does not do what it was supposed to do. Your team is aware, has authority, and has autonomy. With this comes social awareness and responsibility. It means being aware of what people are doing around you, the mistakes they are making. It is not turning a blind eye to poor decisions and/or inaction.

It means seeing behavior, lack of collaboration, lack of integration, and lack of communication and helping those involved become aware. Your team, through their magnanimous behavior, does not get to absolve themselves where they observe obtuse behavior and say, "Oh, but they did so and so."

In stepping up awareness and engagement, your team becomes part of the evangelic heartbeat of the company. This draws them into situations where maintaining the high ground without being obnoxious is critical. You, your peers, and the executive team have no chance of seeing and experiencing the floor interactions the way they do. The adage of, "See something, say something," matters—you need to hold them accountable for this.

They will rise to the occasion; they will like being held accountable. You must help measure their organizational influence, so they are not ostracized.

### Remove Obstacles

Your primary responsibility is to facilitate your team's success by removing obstacles that hinder their progress. You should actively seek out and identify potential hurdles, including red tape, resource shortages, financial limitations, release blockages, communication breakdowns, or technical issues. You should address these obstacles as quickly as you can, securing the necessary resources. Your proactive action demonstrates a commitment to success and immediacy of support.

Encourage your team to bring any challenges they encounter to you as early as possible. Given you have created safe spaces, they know they will not face reprisal or retribution. This includes removing bureaucratic hurdles and resolving interpersonal conflicts. You may also need to address external pressures that distract you from the team's focus.

Ensure your team has all the necessary tools and information to perform their tasks effectively, including adequate training and access to essential technology. They need to have a clear understanding of their roles and responsibilities. Protect your team from unnecessary interruptions and distractions by managing upper management's expectations and filtering non-essential requests. This ensures the team can focus on their core responsibilities and resolutions.

## Social Contracts

Defining social contracts with your team is an important aspect of tight cohesion. By doing so, you establish clear expectations between team members as well as with you. The team will behave as a collective. These contracts are essentially agreements that outline the behavioral norms and commitment between team members. They define responsibilities and mutual commitments of behavior that the team sets its foundation on.

Make sure the social contracts are clearly defined. Use straightforward language that everyone understands, outlining the specific behaviors expected from each team member. Social contracts are simple commitments to one another that provide simple comprehensive commitments of humanity and engagement. These should include work ethics, communication, standards, and collaborative practices. The social contracts should reflect mutual commitments, meaning what you expect from your team and within your team, and what they can expect from you as their leader.

Social contracts are underpinned by company and team values; they do not define or replace them. Social contracts are not behavioral contracts. Base your social contracts on the core values of your team and organization. These might include integrity, respect, accountability, and collaboration. Consider the culture you want to build within your team.

Avoid lengthy and complicated statements, keeping them concise and to the point, ensuring everyone can adhere to them. Ensure that the social contracts are relevant to your team's specific context and needs.

Implement decisively, showing that you are serious about upholding them. The team as a collective should enforce commitments, applying them uniformly to all team members, including yourself.

Social contracts I have held include the following:
- Be the servant, be human, always.
- Do your job—own what you do.

- Don't let any of us get caught with our pants down.
- 6-month resignation window

By clearly defining and implementing social contracts, you set the foundation for a strong, unified team. These agreements help in aligning behaviors with the team's values, fostering a positive work environment.

### Finding Solutions

Empower your team to take accountability for finding solutions. Give them the problem-setting parameters and boundaries, and avoid telling them how to solve them. You want to encourage independent thinking and foster responsibility.

Outline the necessary constraints, like budget and deadline, and leave the solution path open to their creativity. If they miss the mark, conduct a retrospective analysis to understand what went wrong and how to improve. Remember, you own their failures and are responsible for demonstrating your commitment to their development, being the gateway to their creativity and initiative.

Encourage your team to be responsible for their work along with managing and holding one another accountable. Create an environment where debate draws in diverse perspectives and collaboration. Allow them to change work methods if needed.

They will not be able to scale themselves, the team, you, or the company if you orchestrate every move. By stepping back, you enable your team to develop crucial skills in problem-solving and decision-making while building their confidence. Encourage open and honest discussions to identify root causes and prevent future mistakes when the team misses the mark.

Promote peer-to-peer accountability and constructive debate. Encouraging a respectful, challenging culture will lead to well-rounded solutions. This culture of accountability and autonomy builds a self-sustaining team capable of achieving great results independently, enhancing overall company performance and growth.

## Speak Openly and Honestly

Speak openly and honestly about issues within your team. Be as transparent as you can; press the envelope. This applies across company reviews, conflicts, interpersonal issues, priorities, leadership challenges, product launches, and finances.

Being open and honest builds trust and ensures that issues are addressed proactively, preventing them from festering and causing larger problems. Transparent discussions about company performance and challenges help align efforts and expectations; the honesty can lead to actionable insights and improvements that benefit the entire company.

Conflicts are inevitable in any team. How they are handled makes all the difference. Pretending they don't exist or are not happening will just build resentment. Address conflicts directly and constructively, focusing on finding solutions rather than placing blame. Always look to answer, "What do we do now to move on?" By approaching conflicts with a problem-solving mindset, you turn potential disruptions into growth opportunities.

It is crucial to address interpersonal issues openly and empathetically. Encouraging team members to voice their concerns and feelings helps prevent misunderstandings and resentment. This promotes a culture of value and helps team members feel heard.

Encourage team members to speak with the intention of solving problems or generating ideas, shifting the focus from venting frustrations to finding constructive solutions. Make it clear that while it's important to discuss issues, incessant complaining or whining can only create a negative atmosphere and detract from the team's ability to find solutions. Encourage constructive feedback and discussions with clear actions that will lead to positive outcomes.

No issue should be considered above or below you, regardless of whether you have any immediate answers or solutions. You should allow people to talk about their concerns and feel heard. This will release pent-up energies and frustrations and allow team members to feel valued and understood.

Your behavior and how you engage around sensitive topics, how you talk to resolve them, matter.

## Transparency

When you start managing a team, sharing information and keeping everyone in the loop may be a bridge too far. As you gain organizational and team experience and the team evolves, you will need to be discerning about what information to share and with whom. This discernment is crucial to prevent rumors and to protect team members from information they may not be equipped to handle, causing either over or under-reaction.

Not all team members can process or benefit from the same information. Some details, particularly those discussed in executive meetings, may be sensitive or require a level of discretion or extensive elaboration. Your role is to create a direct translation from executive decisions and discussions, from wherever you are in the hierarchy, distilling the information into what is relevant and actionable for your team. When appropriate, brief your team and encourage them to seek out further details.

Regularly update your team on what the company is talking about and deciding. They should not be getting these insights through any other method; this is your responsibility, period. This transparency helps them understand the broader context in which they are operating and how their work fits into the bigger picture. It tells them you have their back and there should be no surprises. Being open about conflicts and challenges the company faces encourages trust and fosters honesty.

Encourage open dialogue in one-on-one settings and group discussions. Be strategic about these conversations and ensure that the environment is conducive to honest and constructive dialogue. By inviting and initiating dialogue, you show that you don't have all the answers and value the input and perspectives of your team.

Share everything you can in your executive briefings with your team, covering topics directly, indirectly, and not related to your team. Keep them updated, and make them feel like a part of the company. This inclusivity helps them feel valued and part of the management process. This approach also helps them understand the reasons behind certain decisions and reduce uncertainty.

Sharing information strategically and fostering an inclusive environment where dialogue is encouraged are essential for effective leadership. By gradually learning what to share and with whom, you protect your team from unnecessary stress while keeping them informed and engaged.

## Trust Them

Trusting your team is foundational for effective leadership. Trust empowers teams; it instills confidence and encourages them to take ownership of their responsibilities. I strongly encourage you to give trust upfront, unconditionally. I do not believe you yield the best out of people by making them earn your trust.

Beginning with trust sets a positive tone and fosters a collaborative environment. Trust should not be something that needs to be earned over time; it should be the default stance at the outset. If you tell your team, "Work with me for twelve months and show me I can trust you," you lose. Most people will lean in when they experience unconditional and unwavering trust.

This approach encourages team members to live up to the trust placed in them and motivates them to retain it through responsible behavior. Starting with trust, you set the stage for team members to take ownership of their actions and the trust they have been given. They need to understand that while they start with trust, retaining it is crucial. This sense of accountability encourages them to act responsibly and maintain the integrity of the information they handle.

Starting with trust is fundamental to effective leadership and team cohesion. By giving your team trust from the outset and emphasizing the importance of retaining it, you create a positive and supportive work environment. Addressing misalignments constructively and fostering open discussions help maintain a respectful and professional atmosphere.

Breaches of trust will occur despite your best efforts. It's important to approach these situations with grace and understand that when team members breach trust, it is often a mistake. Use these moments as learning opportunities to reinforce the importance of confidentiality and trust within the team. Handling missteps will reinforce your leadership strength.

There may well come a time when the trust breach is significant and unrepairable. When this happens, move swiftly, gently, and firmly to move the person on.

## Work-Life Balance

Emphasizing the importance of work-life balance is of the utmost importance. Team members who feel balanced are way more productive, creative, and engaged. Your team will be more willing to go the extra mile when it's truly needed when you demonstrate flexibility and understanding. This reciprocal relationship fosters a strong, supportive environment where the team feels seen.

Embrace hybrid and flexible work arrangements, allowing your team to work remotely and adjust their hours as needed to fit their lifestyle. Be adaptable to different working styles and recognize that productivity thrives in various environments.

Make sure you have hard data that shows over or under work, over or under allocation. Many managers decide not to participate in work effort visibility, with the team bearing the consequences as a result of a void in management information on load and use; the company can only work with what it has available.

Regular breaks through the day, week, month, and year help prevent burnout and maintain productivity. Implement policies that encourage (if not force) breaks, such as a "no meetings" policy. Flexibility allows team members to manage personal responsibilities and reduces stress. Effective time management helps team members balance their workload efficiently. Clear expectations reduce ambiguity and stress about job responsibilities. Communicate pervasively around expectations and deadlines.

Maintain your own work-life balance and show that it's acceptable to disconnect after work hours. Offer resources such as counseling services and stress-management workshops. Recognition and rewards can boost morale and motivate team members. Acknowledge hard work and achievements regularly through formal and informal programs. Encourage teamwork and provide opportunities for professional growth.

You must be vigilantly aware of overload and burnout, especially when you have a highly dedicated and passionate team.

## 360 Reviews

360-degree feedback involves gathering comprehensive performance evaluations from a variety of sources, peers, subordinates, and supervisors. This method provides a holistic view of an individual's performance, capturing different perspectives on their strengths and areas for improvement. To properly benefit from this, you should implement these reviews as an ongoing process versus an annual or bi-annual event. Take interest in your team—every day. Lead and drive them—every day.

Traditional periodic reviews fail to capture the dynamic nature of a team member's performance and development. Rather, they focus on recent activities, missing out on a more balanced and continuous view. I implore you to adopt a persistent interest in your team, engaging in continuous appraisals along with regular check-ins and feedback sessions to ensure you stay attuned to their development.

Show consistent interest in direct and indirect reports through regular informal conversations, covering topics including their goals and obstacles they are facing. By maintaining an ongoing dialogue, you build a stronger understanding of their performance and can provide timely support and feedback.

Encourage a culture where feedback flows freely, creating opportunities for team members to give and receive feedback from a range of people each team member works with. This culture promotes transparency and continuous improvement and helps team members feel more engaged and valued, knowing that their input matters and their development is a priority.

Regular feedback helps team members stay aligned with organizational goals and expectations, allowing for real-time adjustments and ensuring that challenges are addressed promptly rather than waiting for the annual review cycle. This approach fosters a culture of continuous learning and development where team members are constantly improving and adapting.

Adopting a 360-degree feedback approach with continuous appraisals helps in creating a transparent and supportive growth-oriented work environment. By paying persistent interest in your team, you not only stay informed about their progress and challenges but also foster a culture of continuous improvement and mutual respect. This ongoing commitment to feedback and development ensures that your team remains engaged and motivated while being aligned with organizational goals, ultimately driving better performance and success.

## Being Larger

You need to embody and demonstrate larger-than-life qualities while always maintaining the high ground. Communicate high expectations to your team members, encouraging them to exceed their own limitations and step out of their comfort zones to take on new responsibilities. Hold them accountable for their goals and commitments, ensuring they understand the importance of their roles in the team's success.

Integrity and ethical behavior must be evident in all your actions, setting a standard for your team to follow. Ensure fairness and transparency in all decisions and actions, treating all team members equally. Uphold professionalism in interactions with team members, peers, and stakeholders, addressing conflicts promptly and fairly to maintain team cohesion and trust.

Stay ahead of rumors by communicating openly and frequently with your team, addressing misinformation promptly with facts and clarity. If a legitimate issue arises, own it, acknowledge mistakes openly, and take responsibility for resolving them using these moments to improve processes and prevent future occurrences.

Be vigilant in identifying political behavior within the team or organization, encouraging open discussions about any such behavior observed. Establish clear policies that promote transparency and fairness, ensuring decisions are made based on merit. Foster an inclusive culture where everyone feels valued and heard, encouraging collaboration over competition.

Share your engagement strategies and successes with other leaders participating in cross-departmental and cross-functional meetings and forums to discuss effective leadership practices and learn from others. Actively demonstrate your engagement style in various settings, influencing other leaders to adopt similar approaches.

Maintain consistency in your actions and decisions, providing guidance and stability. Be reliable and dependable, following through on your commitments and promises. Be actively present in your team's daily activities, showing that you are involved and invested in their success and exhibiting the behaviors and attitudes you expect from your team.

Encourage a culture of self-regulation where team members hold themselves and each other accountable, reducing the need for constant oversight. Promote peer support and collaboration, making common sense a shared value that spreads quickly.

To implement these principles, provide regular training sessions on leadership communication and conflict resolution to equip your team with the necessary skills. Establish feedback mechanisms such as surveys, suggestion boxes, and open forums to gather input and address concerns promptly. Implement recognition programs that reward behaviors aligning with integrity and accountability while encouraging collaboration. Maintain transparent communication channels to keep everyone informed and engaged, and regularly update the team on goals, progress, and changes. Develop mentorship programs where experienced leaders can guide and support newer leaders in adopting and practicing these principles.

### Own Their Failures

"You own their failures." Period, regardless of significance. You must also take ownership of their failures in settings where their failures are either identified or spoken about. It is important you use the word "we" in the description of who was accountable. Giving your team autonomy and asking them to trust you means you need to cover their backs. You cannot let them experiment and create brilliance and then throw them under the bus. You win by creating an environment where team members feel safe to take risks and learn from their mistakes.

It is critical that when you give them latitude and autonomy, they know they are not going to be hung out to dry when mistakes happen. You owning their failure demonstrates to them that *you are not just their boss*.

Foster an environment where team members feel safe to admit mistakes and discuss failures openly. The psychological safety you have created will encourage transparency and continuous improvement; cultivate a culture where failures are met with constructive analysis and not blame.

Encourage reflection on the failure and understand what went wrong. Provide constructive feedback to help them learn and grow from these experiences. Use failures as opportunities to improve processes, strategies, and workflows. Analyze what could have been done differently and implement changes to prevent similar failures in the future.

Allow your team to take calculated risks. Innovation often comes from experimentation and stepping outside of the comfort zone. Encourage them to try new ideas, even if there's a chance of failure. Understand that failures are valuable learning opportunities. When team members fail, they gain insights and experiences that can lead to better decision-making in the future.

Allowing your team to fail helps build resilience. They learn to cope with setbacks, recover, and continue striving toward their goals. It builds their confidence when team members know they are trusted to take risks and are supported even when they fail. By owning their failures, you enhance individual development which drives innovation and fosters continuous improvement.

It is inevitable you will, at some stage, need to deal with mistakes. In dealing with them, I encourage safe, private spaces. This is where you get to choose how to address this situation and question to resolution, how the mistake happened, and what could have been done differently. This is where your intent and commitment to leadership will be tested and remembered.

My coaching is for you to recognize the mistake has happened and work to figure out how to fix it. Once it is rectified, give the team a breather, not just an hour. Come back and ask, "What can we do to avoid this happening again in the future?" and keep the discussions going in that direction. On every level, I encourage you to avoid, "Who did it?" "Why did you do it?" and "Why didn't you?"

There may be instances where the mistake is of such significance that you need to take disciplinary and/or corrective actions—for these events I implore you to be human, firm, kind, gentle and fast.

## Avoid Golden Children Syndrome

Golden children syndrome occurs when certain team members who are highly productive or closely aligned with leadership receive disproportionate recognition, opportunities, and/or rewards. While it is natural to acknowledge high performers, consistently favoring a select few can lead to significant challenges for these team members: positioning them as "golden children" creates an inevitable divide. While these team members are exceedingly deserving of the recognition, you must measure the veracity with which you give it.

I've been there on multiple occasions in multiple companies and asked my leadership to stop referring to me as the "ideal behavior and team member" use case of expected or normal behavior. The amount of trouble and division this caused is unspeakable.

Some team members will feel undervalued and overlooked, leading to resentment and decreased morale. Favoritism will create divisions within your team, hindering collaboration and cohesion. When only a few voices are consistently heard, the team misses out on diverse perspectives and innovative ideas from other members. Disengaged team members are more likely to seek opportunities elsewhere, leading to higher turnover rates.

Even within highly productive teams, the presence of golden children syndrome is detrimental. High productivity should be a collective achievement, and every team member's contribution should be valued, ensuring all team members experience being recognized and valued to maintain high morale and engagement, which is essential for sustaining productivity.

Diverse input from the whole team fosters innovation and reduces the probability of favoritism, which will stifle creativity and limit the team's potential. Fair and equitable treatment strengthens the team's trust in leadership and the organization, reinforcing a positive work culture. Recognizing all contributions helps in retaining top talent: team members who feel valued are more likely to stay and contribute to the team's success.

## Down Time

You are responsible for ensuring there is a healthy dose of down time for your team. It is your job to track their social and attentive levels and how they reference and talk about their personal worlds. You do this by focusing on results rather than hours worked. You have to trust your autonomous environment and quarterback to ensure your team is giving themselves health and space. You need to emphasize the importance of achieving goals and completing tasks over logging hours.

Trust your team by allowing them to manage their own time. This will increase motivation and work effort. It does not matter what hours they work as long as they are working the sum of their hours, getting their work done, and not causing delays or impacting other teams.

Implement generous leave policies, allowing team members to take the time they need for personal matters and rest. Cater to a range of types of leave, including vacation days, mental health days, and personal leave.

Encourage regular breaks throughout the workdays for team members to recharge and maintain productivity. Offer flexible scheduling options, including compressed workweeks and extra work hours on some days that count toward taking additional time off. Creating extended weekends will boost mental health and well-being.

Clearly defining goals and objectives for each team member ensures they understand what is expected of them. This should cover deliverables and deadlines. Performance metrics that focus on the quality and impact of work rather than the number of hours worked help prioritize tasks by distinguishing between what needs immediate attention and what can wait. This clarity reduces unnecessary stress and allows for better time management.

Show respect for your team's time. This will encourage them to reciprocate when extra effort is needed. This mutual respect builds loyalty and a sense of duty. Establishing clear protocols for emergencies or times when after-hours work is necessary ensures team members understand these situations are exceptions. Ensure only critical projects that require additional hours are assigned for after-hours or weekend work, and ensure that extra work is meaningful and necessary. Allocate resources effectively to prevent team members from being overburdened and help maintain a healthy work-life balance.

Providing clear guidelines on what types of work are considered high priority and require after-hours attention and what can be handled during regular work hours empowers your team to make decisions about their work schedules based on these guidelines. Encouraging them to push back on unnecessary after-hours work helps maintain a balanced and productive work environment.

## Keep Your Instructional Opinion to Yourself

One of the most challenging yet crucial aspects of your approach is to refrain from sharing your instructional opinion or view on how the problem could or should be solved. This means all of them! Regardless of how good or how riddled with holes your intentions are, this includes statements like, "I'm not telling you what to do, but if I was in your seat . . ." and any derivative thereof.

Your insights and experiences are valuable, yet offering your opinion too soon can stifle, if not collapse, creativity and independent thinking. Allow the team to brainstorm and develop their own strategies. This empowers them to take full ownership of the process and outcome and build muscles you will need when you scale or big problems arise. This inevitably means they will absolutely make mistakes. Let them—in safe ways.

Absolutely resist the urge to provide step-by-step instructions. Instead, encourage them to explore various methods and approaches. This will develop critical problem-solving skills as they figure out the solution themselves. The learnings gained from these mistakes are invaluable.

Avoid directing the team on the process or which team members should be involved. Allow them to decide how to approach the problem and who among their colleagues can best contribute to the solution. This encourages collaboration and initiative within the team as members learn to leverage each other's strengths and expertise.

By holding the team accountable for solutions to challenges, you instill a sense of responsibility and ownership. Team members become more engaged and vested in the outcome knowing their efforts directly impact the success of the project. This approach promotes trust and empowerment, where individuals feel valued and capable of making significant contributions.

This encourages continuous learning and development. As team members navigate challenges, they build problem-solving skills and resilience. This enhances the overall capability and agility of the team.

By giving your team the problem, setting parameters, and stepping back, you foster a culture of accountability, innovation, and growth. Empower your team to take ownership of their work. They will rise to the challenge, delivering creative and effective solutions.

## Organizational Dragons

Organizational dragons include behaviors that the team knows exists yet will not talk about. These include:
- Favoritism and unfair treatment (nepotism, cronyism, favoritism, and discrimination),
- Poor management practices (micromanagement,
- Unrealistic expectations, lack of recognition,
- Resistance to change),
- Communication and interpersonal issues (lack of communication,
- Blame culture,
- Exclusionary practices: deliberately excluding certain employees, gossip and rumor-spreading,
- Bullying and harassment), and
- Unethical and unprofessional behavior (retaliation, sabotage, unethical behavior, conflicts of interest).

Facing organizational dragons early and often is crucial for maintaining a healthy and productive environment. These dragons are the underlying issues that, left unaddressed, will erode the foundation of trust, loyalty, and passion within your team. These dragons creep up on you slowly and must be touched on and spoken about as early as you are able. Allowing them to brew will make the effort to rectify them harder and consequences larger.

Perceptions and experiences will significantly impact morale and cohesion. Distrust and resentment will entrench itself if team members perceive favoritism or inequity fueled by a lack of transparency. It is essential to address these perceptions directly and transparently as soon as you become aware of the issue. Solicit regular feedback from your team and take their concerns seriously so you can identify any misperceptions before they become larger issues.

When team members feel victimized, perceived or real, it results in an imbalance and leads to toxicity. Your safe spaces and predictable, fair, transparent characteristics will matter here. Be aware and engage. Acknowledge their feelings and work together to find solutions that restore their sense of fairness and inclusion.

When issues arise, address them directly with the individuals involved, emphasizing the importance of owning their part in the situation and working toward a resolution wherever applicable.

Having discussions and/or addressing perceptions and feelings of victimization, which may include abdication of ownership or non-communicative structures, early and often demonstrates your intent. This proactive approach helps maintain a positive, supportive environment where team members feel respected and motivated to contribute. It reinforces the trust and leadership accountability essential for long-term success.

## Discipline in Private

When you address breaches of social contracts and deliverables in private, you show respect for the individual's dignity. You should do everything you can to allow the team member to save face, prevent public embarrassment, and maintain their self-esteem. Handling issues privately builds trust and helps the team to feel comfortable knowing they will address them discreetly.

Be direct and clear about the breach, explaining what happened and why it is an issue and giving clear expectations moving forward. Provide constructive feedback aimed at improvement and focusing on the behavior or action that needs to change, not on the person's character. Work together to find solutions, discuss ways to prevent similar breaches in the future, and offer support and resources if needed. Develop an action plan with specific steps the team member can take in order to correct the issue, including clear goals and timelines.

Celebrate successes publicly to boost morale and show appreciation for hard work. Acknowledge individual and team achievements in the appropriate forums (meetings, emails, or newsletters). Make sure you provide balanced feedback, including areas for improvement and recognition. Address breaches privately and be part of the successes.

*"They who dare, win!"*

# LET THEM . . .

## Let Them Be

One of your most important roles as a leader is to create an environment where each team member feels free to be themselves and is encouraged to grow into who they really are. This means celebrating their individuality and supporting their personal and professional development.

Encourage your team members to bring their authentic selves to work. You want them to feel comfortable expressing their uniqueness. Diverse voices lead to better outcomes. Your role is to encourage your team members as they discover and develop their strengths. You are responsible for the resources and opportunities they need to pursue their interests and achieve their goals. Work to help them develop confidence and competence in their abilities.

Strive to create safe and inclusive environments where team members feel valued and respected through active listening and acknowledging their contributions. This includes addressing any barriers that might hinder their growth. Inclusivity is key to fostering a sense of belonging and motivation.

Encourage your team members to explore new ideas and take risks. Growth often comes from stepping out of one's comfort zone. You want your teams to feel empowered to try new things. This includes making mistakes along the way or taking the long way round; failures are all learning opportunities.

Each team member has unique aspirations and needs. Work with them to tailor development opportunities that align with their career goals and personal interests.

Make it a point to recognize and celebrate the growth and achievements that boost morale and reinforce the importance of continuous development. Celebrate successes no matter how large or small, encourage ongoing growth, and embolden your team to be themselves. This approach facilitates individual fulfillment along with overall success and resilience.

Your goal is to allow your team to be and become who they are meant to be by fostering authenticity, creating a safe environment, and encouraging growth.

### Let Them Decide

Empowering your team to make decisions is an important aspect of your leadership responsibilities. It fosters independence and accountability while driving confidence.

Present your team with problems to solve and give them clear objectives to achieve. Be strategic about the decisions you delegate. Focus on problems and decisions that will not critically harm the company if things go wrong. Reserve your direct intervention for high-stakes issues that could potentially break the company—delegate as many small problems that need resolving as quickly as you can. This balance allows you to mentor your team in a safe environment without causing damage to the company.

Outline what needs to be accomplished while refraining from dictating how to get there in any way. You want to encourage them to think critically and develop their own strategies.

Allow your team the freedom to figure out the best way to tackle the problems and trust them to make the right decisions based on their knowledge and expertise. This autonomy will empower them and help build decision-making skills.

Support their decisions, even if you may have chosen a different path. It is important to back their choices and provide the resources needed. You demonstrate confidence in their abilities. Show them the benefits of their decisions, and train them on how to analyze outcomes. Help them see and experience the positive impact of their choices. This continuous loop of decision-making is important for self-learning and confidence.

You cannot be omnipresent 24/7 on all matters. It's essential to delegate effectively to ensure the team operates smoothly without your constant oversight. You need to focus on higher-level strategic issues while your team handles day-to-day operations and problem-solving. You need to learn how far you can let them be.

Allowing your team to make decisions fosters a sense of independence and responsibility. It helps them develop the critical thinking and problem-solving skills essential for their professional growth. This approach helps succession planning and skills multiplication.

You empower by delegating. You create an environment where they can grow and thrive. This approach builds decision-making skills and instills a sense of ownership and accountability. Supporting their decisions reinforces your trust in their abilities and motivates them to continue taking initiative. Your team's muscles will grow over time, you will be a multiplier, and your team will be able to focus on broader and more strategic issues.

## Let Them Disagree

Creating space for disagreement is vital as you foster critical thinking and innovation and develop a robust problem-solving capability within your team. Encouraging open dialogue and diverse perspectives ensures that your team does not become complacent or overly reliant on your direction.

You don't want robots who simply follow orders. You win when your team wants to engage in critical thinking. You foster a dynamic and adaptive team capable of tackling complex problems creatively by encouraging critical thinking. Creating a healthy, robust environment for debate and disagreement is crucial. Encourage your team to discuss different viewpoints and challenge each other's ideas. They need to learn to work through conflicts constructively.

Make it clear that no topic is off-limits for discussion. This openness prevents a culture of fear or hesitation where team members might otherwise feel compelled to wait for directives rather than thinking independently. Start by creating a safe environment where team members feel comfortable voicing their opinions. This involves active listening, showing respect for all viewpoints, and responding constructively to feedback.

Model the behavior you want to see. Encourage debate and openly discuss your ideas and decisions with the team. Show that you value different perspectives and are willing to change your mind when presented with compelling arguments.

Introduce structured debates during meetings. Assign roles or perspectives to team members and encourage them to argue different sides of an issue. This will help hone critical thinking skills and demonstrate that disagreement can be productive and enlightening.

Establish regular feedback loops where team members can discuss what is working and what isn't. Regularly asking for their thoughts and opinions helps identify issues early and promote a culture of continuous improvement. Encourage them to question assumptions and consider alternative solutions; develop a habit of thinking critically.

Creating space for disagreement is essential for fostering critical thinking. Open dialogue and diverse opinions are learning opportunities where resilience and adaptability are built.

## Let Them Fail

Allowing your team to experience failure teaches them resilience, problem-solving, and accountability. Start by assigning a mix of tasks that will build their confidence, stretch their abilities, and expose them to potential failures. It's important to create an environment where both success and failure are leveraged as valuable learning experiences.

Task assignment inevitably means they might fail, but you must refrain from stepping in to prevent it. This hands-off approach is essential for their growth. Find ways to force them to rely on their own problem-solving skills—go on vacation.

While it's important to let them navigate challenges independently, always be ready to catch them when they fall. Think of yourself as the trapeze net for your team, giving them every opportunity to fly and be magnificent and always being there when they fall.

Make sure that team members take ownership of their tasks and their failures. Allowing them to fail means giving them responsibility and holding them accountable for their work. When they encounter failure, walk them through the failure points and help them understand the decisions they made and the consequences of those decisions—this reflection is critical for their development. Encourage them to reflect and introspect to understand their strengths and weaknesses.

Resist the urge to interfere. The team will never learn to handle challenges independently if you or other senior leaders keep stepping in to solve problems. They need to figure out hard answers on their own, including learning how to work together effectively. Allowing your team to fail and learn from those failures is essential for their development. This process helps them build resilience and develop problem-solving skills.

This approach helps develop essential skills and prepares them to handle future challenges.

### Let Them Debate

It's essential to understand the value of allowing your team members to engage in healthy conflict and discourse. One of your key responsibilities as a leader is to create an environment where your team feels safe to express differing opinions and challenge each other's ideas. This requires engaging in robust discourse. It is important to experience that people will not always agree with you, and to navigate through the discourse with composure and professionalism.

You should actively encourage open dialogue and let them know that it's okay to disagree and that their opinions are valued. You want them to feel comfortable voicing their thoughts, including contradicting yours. Open communication is essential for uncovering new perspectives and fostering innovation.

The importance of healthy, respectful disagreement cannot be emphasized enough. By keeping discussions professional and respectful, we ensure that conflicts remain constructive and do not escalate into unproductive arguments. By encouraging one another to question assumptions and explore different solutions, we find the best possible outcomes for our projects.

Critical thinking is a skill I value highly, and I believe it is strengthened through healthy discourse and debate.

While you should encourage your team to resolve conflicts among themselves, you should always be available to step in and guide the conversation if needed. Your role is to ensure that the discourse remains productive and that all voices are heard. Help mediate when necessary, ensuring the team is focused on finding solutions and not blame.

You should view disagreements as learning opportunities. After any significant conflict, encourage your team to reflect on the experience. What did they learn? How can they improve communication and decision-making processes? This reflection helps the team grow stronger and prepares them for future challenges.

Allowing your team to engage in healthy conflict and discourse is crucial for your success. By letting team members debate and have discourse, you create a culture of open communication and continuous improvement.

## Let Them Lead

It is essential for you to empower your team to take on leadership roles, whether it's leading their own teams or managing projects. Fostering leadership at all levels not only enhances your overall performance, but it contributes to individual growth and development.

One of your primary responsibilities is to create an environment where leadership is cultivated. Encourage your team members to step up and lead their own teams and projects. This empowerment is crucial for their personal growth and the collective success of your company.

Place a high level of trust in your team members' abilities to lead. Whether they are managing their own teams or heading up projects, trust them to make the right decisions and guide their teams effectively. This trust is foundational.

Look for opportunities to assign leadership roles as new projects arise, continuously identifying those who are ready for the challenge. Ensure objectives and expectations are clearly defined, providing the necessary context and goals. Set the parameters within which they need to operate.

Make yourself available to provide ongoing guidance, and be as hands-on as you can so that they feel like they have the autonomy to make decisions. Encourage your team members to figure out the best ways to achieve their goals, leveraging the resources they have at their disposal. This balance of guidance and self-autonomy is critical for fostering leaders.

When team members successfully lead their teams or projects, ensure their achievements are recognized and failures are treated as learning opportunities. By allowing team members to lead, you help them grow, which in turn drives the overall performance, so empower your people to lead teams and projects with trust, clear communication, support, and a focus on continuous development.

### Let Them Own Their Successes

Helping a team and its members own their successes involves creating an environment where they feel responsible and recognized for their contributions. Outline the team's goals and individual responsibilities, ensuring everyone understands how their work contributes to the overall success of the organization. Use the most relevant measurement framework (SMART, OKR, KPI) to set clear goals and provide your team with clear direction and purpose.

Assign tasks and projects that align with skills and career aspirations and have them take full ownership. Give them the authority to make decisions and trust them to achieve their objectives. Acknowledge their achievements and celebrate milestones.

Recognize and reward accomplishments. Organize team-building activities to strengthen relationships. Encourage shared success where the team collectively owns their achievements. By doing this, you create an environment where your team feels responsible, recognized, and valued.

### Let Them Rally

Allowing your team to rally in jest about you is a powerful indicator of strong team cohesion and deep bonds. When your team feels comfortable enough to joke around and tease you, it shows that they trust you and see you as approachable, and it contributes to the overall camaraderie.

When your team feels free to joke around and tease you, it is a sign that they see you as part of the group rather than an unapproachable authority figure. This interaction breaks down hierarchical barriers and creates a relaxed, open environment where team members feel safe to express themselves. It signifies they are comfortable and secure in their roles, and it helps to strengthen the sense of community within the team.

It also signifies that the team has developed its own identity, characterized by mutual respect and trust. When your team can laugh together, especially at your expense, it demonstrates that they are united and feel a collective ownership of the team's culture.

Encouraging this kind of behavior helps to humanize you as a leader and make you more relatable. It shows that you don't take yourself too seriously and that you value the informal, human side of life. It humanizes you as a leader and fosters a relaxed, open, and cohesive team environment.

## Let Them Read

One of the most impactful ways you can affect people's lives is by helping them introspect. You do this by encouraging them to read—wide and pervasively. This practice not only enhances their knowledge and skills but also promotes a culture of continuous learning. Most importantly, it facilitates private reflection and introspection, uninfluenced by you or the company. There is nothing like reading the truth of oneself in a book that has nothing to do with you.

Make reading an integral part of their personal development plans. Use this as informal or formal development. Discuss their reading goals during performance reviews and check-ins. Set clear expectations regarding topics they should be reading and their progress. Each team member will have a different trajectory.

Create a book list that includes foundational texts on various topics important to you. This list should cover areas such as personal development, business acumen, leadership, and skills relevant to your industry. Some foundational books should include titles like *The Trusted Advisor* by David H. Maister, *How to Win Friends and Influence People* by Dale Carnegie, and *Leaders Eat Last* by Simon Sinek.

While a rich curated list is a great starting point, each team member should also have a personalized reading assignment that aligns with their individual goals and interests. Work with them to identify books that will help them grow in their specific roles and address their unique challenges and aspirations.

Encourage your team to explore books that inspire personal growth, such as *Atomic Habits* by James Clear or *Mindset* by Carol S. Dweck. These books can enhance their mindset and improve their overall well-being.

Business and leadership books are essential for developing strategic thinking and managerial skills. Encourage your team to read classics like *Good to Great* by Jim Collins and *The Lean Startup* by Eric Ries. These books offer valuable insights into building and leading successful organizations.

Allocate time during performance reviews to discuss the books your team members are reading. Ask them to share key takeaways and how they plan to apply what they've learned to their work. This practice reinforces the importance of reading and helps them integrate new knowledge into their roles.

Assign each team member two to three books to read per review cycle. Encourage them to seek out new titles that pique their interest and align with their career goals.

At the end of it all, the decision to grow and develop lies with each individual. You instill a sense of responsibility and a desire for self-improvement within your team in driving this. They must want to learn and grow; there is no substitute for intrinsic motivation.

*"The best executive is the one who has sense enough to pick good men to do what he wants done, and self-restraint to keep from meddling with them while they do it."*
—THEODORE ROOSEVELT

# DON'T . . .

I cannot emphasize enough how vital it is to avoid certain detrimental behaviors. Building relationships and establishing credibility takes significant time and effort, often spanning months or even years. A single misstep can undo all that hard work in a matter of minutes.

Trust and credibility are the cornerstones of effective leadership and strong team dynamics. They are built through consistent, honest, and fair interactions. These elements foster a positive and productive work environment once established. They are incredibly fragile and can be shattered by careless actions or words, especially where repeated.

The repercussions are immediate and severe when you engage in behaviors that undermine trust. This happens when you make hasty judgments or fail to follow through on commitments. These actions signal to your team that you are unreliable or unfair. This will lead to a breakdown in trust, the damage of which will take a long time to repair, if at all.

Establishing strong relationships with your team members is a gradual process. It involves getting to know them, understanding their strengths and weaknesses, and consistently supporting them in their roles. This process requires many of the topics covered in this book. Each human interaction contributes to the foundation of trust and mutual respect.

A single negative action can quickly unravel all of your efforts. Be smart! For example, publicly criticizing a team member, breaking a promise, or acting with bias can cause immediate and lasting harm and send deep trust rifts into your team.

Given enough energy, these ripples can affect team morale, engagement, and productivity, causing the exact opposite of everything discussed in this book. The importance of maintaining trust and credibility cannot be overstated. It's your responsibility to ensure that your actions align with your values and the trust your team places in you.

## Don't Judge

This principle is fundamental to creating a positive, inclusive, and supportive work environment. Judging will quickly erode trust and morale, leading to disengagement and a lack of motivation.

It can be a default human nature to make quick judgments, especially when things go wrong or someone makes a mistake. You should consciously resist this temptation. Instead, take a step back and seek to understand the context and reasons behind a person's actions.

Make it a point to never judge, jury, or convict your team members, or for that matter anyone in the company or your personal world.

> *"In your best and worst moments, you are no better or worse than anyone else."*

Publicly criticizing or judging someone will be incredibly damaging to their confidence and can create a toxic team atmosphere. Handle feedback and course corrections privately, focusing on the behavior, not the person.

Strive toward fairness in all interactions and decisions. This means giving everyone a fair chance to explain their side of the story, considering all perspectives before making decisions, and being consistent in how you treat your team. Fairness builds trust and respect, essential components of a high-performing team.

When people feel judged, they are less likely to take risks or share their ideas. This creates a barrier to open communication and stifles innovation.

Focus on proactive leadership instead of judging. This involves setting clear expectations and providing regular feedback and resources to help your team succeed. You reduce the likelihood of issues arising that might lead to judgment by getting in front of the behavior you seek to cultivate. It's about leading with intention and foresight rather than reacting negatively to situations after they occur.

You contribute to building a positive and inclusive team culture by refraining from judgment. This should be a core principle you hold.

## Don't Manipulate

Manipulation is when someone is influencing or controlling another person's thoughts, behaviors, or actions for their own gain and/or to the detriment of that or other team members. This can happen in various forms, such as emotional manipulation, gaslighting, or coercion. Manipulation often involves deceptive tactics and can leave the victim feeling confused, powerless, and unsure of their own thoughts and feelings.

Manipulating someone is generally considered unethical and harmful for several reasons. Manipulation often involves deceit or coercion, which undermines the trust between individuals. Broken trust is challenging to rebuild, affecting both personal and professional relationships. For instance, a leader who manipulates team members to achieve personal goals will erode the trust within the team.

Manipulation typically bypasses the other person's informed consent and exploits their vulnerabilities. This is inherently disrespectful and violates the principle of autonomy, such as convincing someone to take on extra work without informing them of the true workload or consequences.

There are many ways in which someone can be manipulated. Emotional manipulation involves using guilt, fear, or other emotions to manipulate someone into doing or feeling a certain way. Gaslighting is a form of manipulation where the manipulator makes the victim doubt their own memories, perceptions, purpose, and/or sanity. Coercion involves using threats or force to make someone comply with their demands.

Being manipulative involves exploiting vulnerabilities, such as insecurities or past traumas. It can also happen in subtle and gradual manners, making it difficult for the victim to realize they are being manipulated until it's too late.

The psychological impact of manipulation can be significant. It can cause emotional harm to the person being manipulated, leading to feelings of betrayal, guilt, self-doubt, and questioning, and decreased self-esteem. Manipulation also removes an individual's ability to make their own informed decisions, leading to a sense of helplessness and dependency. This is evident when someone is manipulated into making a decision that benefits the manipulator rather than themselves.

Social and professional consequences are also notable. Manipulation can severely damage personal and professional relationships. People are less likely to trust or collaborate with someone they perceive as manipulative, such as colleagues avoiding working with a manipulative coworker, leading to isolation and reduced teamwork. Being known as a manipulator can damage your reputation, with long-term consequences for your career and social standing.

Manipulation is generally seen as morally wrong because it involves deceit and exploitation, going against the principles of fairness, honesty, and respect. Certain forms of manipulation can lead to legal consequences, especially in professional settings. This can include charges of fraud, coercion, or harassment.

A leader who manipulates their team may struggle with guilt and a loss of self-respect. Manipulative behavior can become a habitual way of interacting with others, perpetuating a cycle of negative behavior and relationships. Continually using manipulation to achieve goals can lead to increasingly harmful tactics and further alienation from others.

Effective leadership and healthy relationships are built on transparency, mutual respect, and ethical behavior, all of which are undermined by manipulation.

## Don't Publicly Reprimand

Public reprimands are an absolute no-no. There is no valid reason or excuse for reprimanding a team member in front of their peers. The impact of such actions can be profoundly negative, resulting in a loss of trust and respect among your team members.

Public reprimands humiliate and demoralize the individual being criticized. This affects their confidence and performance and sends a message to the entire team that their work environment is unsafe. It creates an atmosphere of fear and anxiety, stifling creativity and collaboration. The respect and trust you have built with your team will quickly erode.

Reprimanding a team member is not limited to overt actions or harsh words. It can also manifest through subtler cues in body language, tone of voice, facial expressions, and inflections. A disapproving look or condescending tone can be interpreted as a reprimand. It is crucial to be aware of these non-verbal forms of communication and manage them carefully to avoid inadvertently reprimanding someone publicly.

If you find yourself unable to manage your response to failure constructively, step back and remove yourself from the situation temporarily. Reacting in the heat of the moment can lead to unintentional reprimands that harm both the individual and the team. Collect your thoughts and approach the situation with a calm demeanor.

Focus on the behavior or action that needs improvement rather than the person's character. Provide specific feedback and collaborate on finding solutions to prevent similar issues in the future. This method fosters a supportive environment where team members feel valued and motivated to improve.

It's important to cultivate emotional intelligence to manage your responses to failures and mistakes. This involves being self-aware, controlling your impulses, and demonstrating empathy toward your team members. By practicing emotional intelligence, you can respond to challenges in a way that supports growth and development rather than causing harm.

## Don't Embarrass

One of the fundamental principles you must adhere to is never to embarrass your team members. Embarrassment can cause profound and lasting damage to an individual's self-esteem and relationship with you. It is essential to differentiate between being part of someone's problems or failure versus being part of their embarrassment.

Embarrassing someone will have immediate and severe negative effects, including feelings of shame, humiliation, and resentment. A team member who has been embarrassed will become less engaged, motivated, and willing to take risks or share ideas.

It's natural for team members to face challenges and failures; your role is to support them through these times, not to exacerbate their difficulties by causing embarrassment. Being part of their challenge means offering guidance, support, and constructive feedback to help them overcome obstacles. Being part of their embarrassment, on the other hand, means putting them in a situation where they feel exposed and humiliated, which is counterproductive to their growth and your team's cohesion.

Team members are more likely to feel valued and understood when mistakes are handled privately and constructively. They will be more open to feedback and motivated to improve.

Practicing emotional intelligence is crucial in avoiding embarrassing your team members. This involves being aware of your own emotions, understanding the impact of your actions on others, and managing your responses thoughtfully. By demonstrating empathy and respect, you can navigate challenging situations without causing embarrassment.

Embarrassment can cause lasting damage to an individual's confidence and trust in you. Focus on being part of their challenge or failure by offering support and constructive feedback. Avoiding embarrassment preserves the trust and respect you have built, fostering a positive and supportive team environment.

# FINAL WORDS

## Bullies

*My hot button*

Maintaining a healthy work environment is paramount. It is absolutely critical that team members work hard and fast, regardless of who they are, the title they hold, and the skills they have, so it is necessary to get rid of team members identified as bullies who have been addressed for their behavior and chose to continue their behavior.

For this, I define a bully as a team member who displays passive or active aggressive behavior, leverages intimidation tactics to make team members around them lesser than they are, and actively weaponizes information in an ongoing fashion in an effort to demonize or vilify other team members.

You need to get rid of these people immediately. There is nothing that condones this behavior, and the longer you facilitate it, the more you damage any vision, intent, or culture you are trying to create.

These individuals create a toxic atmosphere, causing stress and discomfort among employees. Removing such negative influences helps foster a positive and supportive culture, which is essential for the overall well-being of the workforce.

Protecting team morale and productivity is vital. Team members are more motivated and productive in a respectful and encouraging environment. High morale also reduces team member turnover, helping to retain valuable talent.

When team members feel safe and valued, they are more likely to be engaged and committed to their work, leading to better performance and productivity.

Safeguarding your and your company's reputation is critical. A positive work environment enhances reputations, attracting top talent and clients. It shows that the company values integrity and respect, which can be a significant factor in building a strong employer brand. This, in turn, can lead to better recruitment and retention of high-quality employees, as well as improved customer and client relationships.

Ensuring legal and ethical compliance is another important aspect. Addressing abusive behavior helps prevent potential lawsuits related to harassment or a hostile work environment. Upholding ethical standards reinforces the company's commitment to fairness and respect. By taking a firm stance against such behavior, you demonstrate that your company is serious about maintaining a safe and respectful workplace.

Enhancing team dynamics is crucial for overall success. A harmonious workplace fosters better collaboration and teamwork. When employees feel respected and supported, they are more likely to work well together and contribute to a positive team dynamic. This can lead to increased creativity and innovation, as team members feel more comfortable sharing ideas and taking risks.

By removing bullies, emotional abusers, leeches, and troublemakers, you ensure the well-being of your team members, enhance productivity, and uphold the integrity and reputation of your company. This proactive approach creates a positive, supportive, and legally compliant work environment that benefits both the employees and the organization.

I cannot emphasize the impact and price you will pay to "see if they will change behavior." They will not. Get rid of them immediately.

## Victim Mode
*My weak point*

I try to rise above nearly all situations, but the one I really battle with is where someone willfully, intentionally, persistently, and wantingly keeps themselves in victim mode. While it appears to be the diametric opposite of the bully – its desired outcome is exactly the same as the bully; however, the toxins and resulting organizational disfunction is exactly the same.

As a leader, you can go only so far in trying to help someone who is deeply embroiled in this, to which point that person has to want to change. When you find these people, your job is to help them be self-aware of their self-induced state. Provide facts, insights, and awareness and be patient. They will find themselves eventually.

For clarity, "victim mode" refers to a mindset or behavioral pattern where an individual perceives themselves as a perpetual victim of circumstances, events, or the actions of others. This state of mind is characterized by feelings of helplessness, powerlessness, and a lack of control over one's life. It often involves attributing personal setbacks or negative experiences to external forces rather than recognizing one's role in these situations. While legitimate victimization exists, victim mode is more about a chronic, self-perpetuating way of thinking that impacts one's overall outlook and behavior.

**Characteristics of Victim Mode**
- *External lack of control*: Individuals in victim mode typically believe that their life is controlled by external factors rather than their own actions. They often feel that life happens to them and that they have little influence over outcomes.
- *Blame and excuses*: There is a tendency to blame others for personal problems or failures. This might include blaming friends, family, colleagues, society, or even fate. Excuses are frequently made to justify why things cannot improve or why certain actions cannot be taken.
- *Negative self-talk*: A person in victim mode engages in negative self-talk, reinforcing their feelings of inadequacy and powerlessness. Phrases like "I can't do anything right," or, "This always happens to me," are common.
- *Pessimism and fatalism*: A pervasive sense of pessimism about the future and a belief that bad things are bound to happen characterize this mindset. This fatalistic view can lead to a lack of motivation to try to change circumstances.

- *Passive behavior*: Rather than taking proactive steps to address challenges, individuals in victim mode often adopt a passive approach. They wait for others to solve their problems or for circumstances to change on their own.
- *Seeking sympathy and validation*: There is often a strong need for sympathy and validation from others. Sharing their struggles repeatedly, they seek affirmation of their victim status, which can create a cycle of dependency on external validation.

### Breaking Out of Victim Mode
- *Self-awareness and reflection*: Recognizing the pattern of victim thinking is the first step. Self-reflection and awareness can help identify when one is falling into this mindset.
- *Taking responsibility*: Shifting to an internal focus of control, where one acknowledges their role in situations and takes responsibility for their actions, can be empowering.
- *Positive action and problem-solving*: Developing proactive problem-solving skills and taking positive action can help break the cycle. Setting small, achievable goals can build confidence and a sense of control.
- *Seeking support*: Professional help, such as therapy or counseling, can be beneficial in addressing deep-seated patterns of victim thinking and developing healthier coping mechanisms.

## Remote vs. Hybrid

I understand the significant push and support for remote work. It has been widely perceived to increase productivity and provide a flexible work environment that accommodates various personal and professional needs. There have also been reports that state a net zero increase or decrease in productivity.

The flexibility remote work offers allows individuals to navigate their days efficiently, balancing work and life seamlessly. I believe that a full remote work model comes with substantial drawbacks that can impact team dynamics, organizational culture, and long-term growth.

While I recognize the benefits of remote work, I firmly support a hybrid model, which I define as requiring team members to be in the office at least two days a week. This balance allows us to reap the advantages of remote work while mitigating its downsides. Here's why I advocate for a hybrid approach:

One of the most significant impacts of full remote work is the nature of relationships it fosters. Remote work relies heavily on Zoom and other virtual communication tools, which can limit our interactions to purely professional contexts. In such settings, we know people for their skills and the work they do, but we miss out on understanding them as whole individuals. Face-to-face interactions provide a richer context for relationships, enabling us to gain insights into each other's personalities, values, and motivations.

In a remote environment, we miss out on the natural human learning that occurs through casual interactions. The spontaneous conversations that happen in office kitchens and hallways and during lunch breaks are invaluable. These informal exchanges facilitate knowledge sharing, mentorship, and the organic spread of ideas. They also help in building a sense of camaraderie and community within the team, which is hard to replicate in a fully remote setup.

Remote work can obscure the nuances of communication, making it difficult to detect differing interpretations and misunderstandings. In face-to-face settings, body language, tone, and immediate feedback play a crucial role in ensuring clarity and alignment. Virtual meetings, while effective for many purposes, often lack these subtleties, leading to potential misalignments and assumptions that go unchecked. This is particularly concerning for complex projects that require close collaboration and precise coordination.

Another significant drawback of full remote work is the challenge it poses in identifying and nurturing emerging leaders. Leadership potential is often observed through human interaction, problem-solving in real-time, and the ability to influence and motivate others in person. Remote work tends to emphasize technical proficiency over interpersonal skills, which can lead to appointing leaders based solely on their technical abilities rather than their overall leadership potential.

Succession planning becomes more difficult in a remote setting. The lack of face-to-face interactions and the transient nature of remote work can result in senior leadership moving between companies more frequently. This constant movement disrupts natural succession growth and makes it harder to cultivate long-term loyalty and commitment to the organization.

In a remote work environment, gossip and negative talk can become rife and challenging to address. The absence of regular, informal check-ins means that these issues can fester unnoticed. When everyone is dispersed, it's harder to pinpoint the source of negative sentiment and address it effectively. In contrast, a hybrid model allows for more opportunities to gauge team morale and intervene before issues escalate.

I acknowledge that this is a contentious topic and that opinions on remote versus hybrid work can vary widely. As we navigate these changes, time will reveal the challenges and solutions for integrating remote work effectively. It is essential to remain adaptable and open to evolving our work models to suit both organizational needs and team member well-being.

While full remote work offers many advantages, a hybrid model strikes a better balance by combining the flexibility of remote work with the benefits of in-person interactions. This approach supports stronger relationships, better communication, and more effective leadership development. By maintaining a hybrid work environment, we can foster a cohesive, innovative, and resilient organization that thrives in both virtual and physical spaces.

## Closing

It is essential to empower your team by trusting them to handle their responsibilities. They were hired for their skills and expertise, so let them utilize those abilities. Your primary role is to identify and remove any barriers that might prevent your team from performing their tasks efficiently. This could be logistical issues, resource shortages, or inter-departmental conflicts. Once you have provided the necessary resources and removed obstacles, step back and allow your team to work independently. Micromanaging will hinder creativity and productivity.

Ensure your team knows that they can come to you with questions or for guidance by maintaining an open-door policy and explicitly communicating your availability and willingness to help. Regularly remind them that you are there for support, not to control. If a team member lacks certain knowledge or skills, offer to teach them or provide resources for their learning. This not only helps them grow but also builds a stronger, more competent team. Leverage your experience to guide your team by sharing your insights and lessons learned to help them navigate challenges effectively.

You can adopt either a doer-leader or leader-doer style. As a doer-leader, you actively participate in the work while also providing leadership, showing your team how things are done through your actions. As a leader-doer, you focus on guiding your team, setting goals, and removing obstacles first, then you take on tasks that others might avoid or need additional support with. It is important to find a balance between doing the work and leading effectively. Being too involved in the day-to-day tasks can distract from strategic planning and team support.

In summary, empowering your team, removing obstacles, stepping back to allow autonomy, maintaining open communication, providing guidance, and balancing your role are key to creating a productive and motivated team while also fulfilling your responsibilities as a leader.

*Remember:*

*Indecision is a decision.*
*Inaction is action.*

# BE MAGNANIMOUS

Ok, that was a long-winded way of telling you that while theory is important, people matter. How you find people, love them, engage with them, be human with them, draw the best out of them, is about being human with them and engaging with your team like you would your children and or siblings.

Being Magnanimous is not tangibly hard to do, its quite easy in fact. Being continuously self-aware and people around-you-aware can be emotionally taxing and draining until you teach yourself.

I have had a wonderful journey learning from my coaches and mentors – all of them have been personal friends, none of them have been paid. I have had the privilege to work with some wonderful people (and some idiots) - I choose to celebrate the greatness of people and walk away from the idiots.

I could not isolate in any order any of the traits I have covered here. In my mind they are all critically important for the team. It does NOT mean you need to do them, yes – they will help, if something does not naturally fall within your capabilities, don't fight it, delegate it, and tell people you have delegated.

Every day you slide your foot onto the floor out of bed you decide your day! Only you decide the consequence, value, and outcome of the day – nobody else. Every time a team member does something brilliant or stupid, every time some praise or reprimand is due, you get to decide, you get to act, you get to be Magnanimous – or not! You get to decide how much love and energy you are willing to give or receive, you and you alone.

Your team need you, you need you. Leverage the theories and foundations, trust your gut and team, be human. Start with how you want to be known, what kind of team you want to lead, and how you want your team to see you.

Work backward from there: identify traits you are great at and start practicing them immediately. Pull your team together and tell them what you are trying to do and why; paint them the picture you have for your leadership style. Then frequently reflect on the status of your growth by yourself, with your teams, and with your leaders.

Don't ever stop developing yourself, read, read, read, listen, watch, listen, watch, learn. Find a mentor or a coach for yourself. Leverage personal life coaches to help with character development and professional mentors for career progression. Be graceful with yourself, and give yourself time to get there.

If you are battling to find your feet of what kind of leader you want to be or are, get some direct leadership development coaching from professionals such as BoostLearning online[2].

You go find you, own yourself. Decide who you are, engage through this book, come back to it often, mark it up, fold the pages, scratch text out. Engage with yourself honestly. I would love to hear about your stories, how you make this real, tell me where I got it wrong. What's your journey to becoming Magnanimous? Get past pure heart and intent, and get to the core of human leadership.

---

2 https://www.boostlearning.online/contact/interest
a platform designed to enhance the capabilities and confidence of managers and leaders. It focuses on practical development rather than traditional training, offering resources, tools, and podcasts aimed at improving management skills in real-world contexts. The platform provides various programs and solutions to help managers lead their teams effectively, foster accountability, and delegate tasks efficiently

*Go find the you you were designed
and meant to be, and leave the you
you were taught to be behind*

# MAGNANIMOUS

- **Magnanimous**: noble, generous, forgiving
- **Greathearted**: kind, noble, selfless
- **Noble**: high character, elevated deeds
- **Generous**: free from pettiness, big-hearted
- **Unselfish**: giving of oneself
- **Forgiving**: tolerant, understanding
- **Charitable**: open-handed, unstinting
- **High-minded**: noble sensibility
- **Bountiful**: munificent, ungrudging

*Be Magnificent.*

*Be Magnanimous!!*

# BOOKS I RELY ON

## My mandatory reading list:

- *Trusted Advisor* –David H. Maister
- *Good to Great* –Jim Collins
- *Radical Candor* –Kim Scott
- *Crucial Conversations* –Kerry Patterson
- *No Excuses!* –Brian Tracy
- *Influencer* –Kerry Patterson, Joseph Grenny, David Maxfield
- *Atomic Habits* –James Clear
- *Pitch Anything* –Oren Klaff
- *Unleash the Power Within* –Tony Robbins

## Personal Development

- *Designing Your Life* –Bill Burnett
- *Digital Body Language* –Erica Dhawan
- *Impact Players* –Liz Wiseman
- *Lean In* –Sheryl Sandberg
- *Mindset* –Carol Dweck
- *Think Again* –Adam Grant
- *The 6 Types of Working Genius* –Patrick M. Lencioni
- *The Digital Mindset* –Paul Leonardi
- *The ONE Thing* –Gary Keller
- *Traction* –Gino Wickman

- *You Just Don't Understand* –Deborah Tannen
- *Stop Overreacting* –Judith Siegel PhD LCSW
- *Stop Overthinking Your Life* –Camryn Kelley
- *Blink: The Power of Thinking Without Thinking* –Malcolm Gladwell
- *Daring Greatly* –Brené Brown
- *10x Is Easier Than 2x* –Dan Sullivan, Dr. Benjamin Hardy
- *Know What You're For* –Jeff Henderson, John C. Maxwell
- *How to Win Friends and Influence People* –Dale Carnegie

## Leadership books

- *Leaders Eat Last: Why Some Teams Pull Together and Others Don't* –Simon Sinek
- Team of Teams: New Rules of Engagement for a Complex World
- *Never Split the Difference* –Chris Voss, Tahl Raz
- *Dare to Lead* –Brene Brown
- *Everybody Matters* –Bob Chapman
- *Go Slow to Grow Fast* –Brent R. Tilson
- *Good Leaders Ask Great Questions* –John Maxwell
- *How to Be a Great Boss* –Gino Wickman, René Boer
- *Be a Better Team by Friday* –Justin Follin, David Butlein Greenspan
- *Multipliers, Revised* –Liz Wiseman, Stephen Covey—foreword

## Business

- *Blue Ocean Strategy* –W. Chan Kim, Renee Mauborgne
- *Change Anything* –Kerry Patterson, Joseph Grenny, David Maxfield, Ron McMillan, Al Switzler
- *Start with Why* –Simon Sinek
- *Measure What Matters* –John Doerr
- *The Lean Startup* –Eric Ries

# ABOUT THE AUTHOR

*Here lies someone who cared!*

Andrew Brummer is a strategic business advisor and operational leader who combines deep technical expertise with broad business acumen. As a first-generation immigrant to the USA, he brings a unique global perspective shaped by extensive experience across Africa, Europe, the UK, Canada, Central America, and 47 US states.

Andrew's superpower lies in finding efficiency and effectiveness in nearly everything and everyone. He excels at pulling the best out of people and driving toward shared consciousness while maintaining an intuitive sense of the most efficient path toward outcomes. His focus remains on optimizing the use of time and money while serving as a natural multiplier in organizations.

His expertise spans business operations, organizational change, IT service management, business process optimization, sales operations, intellectual property management, and startup advisory. Andrew's leadership style centers on creating autonomous teams, driving efficient use of resources, and building strong cultural foundations.

Andrew's commitment to paying it forward has created global impact through mentoring and coaching across the Middle East, Africa, Caribbean Islands, Europe, UK, Central America, Canada, and USA. He actively volunteers with organizations including TiE Atlanta, Access Foundation, and various startup incubators.

Family stands at the center of Andrew's world. When not transforming businesses, he channels his creativity into programming 35,000+ Christmas lights synchronized to 220+ songs, crafting live-edge wood furniture, and operating Sparky's Reef Farm with his son, breeding marine sea life.

Today, Andrew serves as a fractional executive, mentor, and advisor, helping:

- Facilitation: Strategic and Business
- CEO and executive whisperer
- Advisor, mentor, and coach
- Drive efficient use of time and money
- Build strong cultural foundations
- Create autonomous, self-sustaining teams

# CONNECT WITH ANDREW

The Ardunan Village:
www.ardunan.com

Book website
www.leadingmagnanimously.com

Email:
andrew@leadingmagnanimously.com

LinkedIn:
https://www.linkedin.com/in/andrewbrummer/

Whether you're a founder seeking guidance, a leader looking to scale, or someone passionate about operational excellence, Andrew welcomes meaningful connections and conversations that create value.

# A free ebook edition is available with the purchase of this book.

**To claim your free ebook edition:**
1. Visit MorganJamesBOGO.com
2. Sign your name CLEARLY in the space
3. Complete the form and submit a photo of the entire copyright page
4. You or your friend can download the ebook to your preferred device

A **FREE** ebook edition is available for you or a friend with the purchase of this print book.

CLEARLY SIGN YOUR NAME ABOVE

**Instructions to claim your free ebook edition:**
1. Visit MorganJamesBOGO.com
2. Sign your name CLEARLY in the space above
3. Complete the form and submit a photo of this entire page
4. You or your friend can download the ebook to your preferred device

## Print & Digital Together Forever.

Snap a photo   Free ebook   Read anywhere

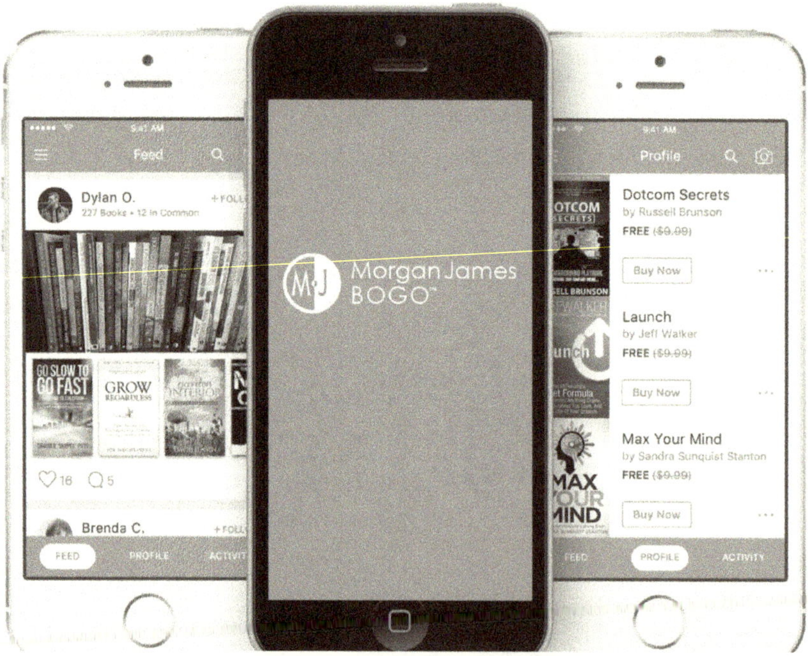

www.ingramcontent.com/pod-product-compliance
Lightning Source LLC
Jackson TN
JSHW020904110525
84066JS00002B/5